Praise for *United States v. George W. Bush et al.*

"On the basis of the evidence presented by former prosecutor Elizabeth la Vega, I'm convinced that George Bush, Dick Cheney, Donald Rumsfeld and their fellow 'indictees' are fully entitled to a fair and honest trial—indeed, several fair and honest trials—by juries of their peers."

—DANIEL ELLSBERG, former State and Defense Department official who revealed the Pentagon Papers

"De la Vega has accomplished an amazing feat with this singularly triumphant presentation of the intersection between political fantasy and legal reality. Reading the delightfully logical and clearheaded *United States v. George W. Bush et al.* is both incredibly sobering, and yet strangely hopeful. Real American patriots can only wish the United States godspeed in this case, and this brief is destined to be well studied by principals in all three branches of American government, as well as by those who serve as the Fourth Estate."

—KAREN KWIATKOWSKI, retired U.S. Air Force Lieutenant Colonel

"What a great book. In the form of a fictional grand jury looking into criminal charges of conspiracy and fraud committed by the Bush administration concerning the war on Iraq, this book contains the documented details of public comments and secret actions of President Bush and his senior advisors in the year prior to the war.

"The Department of Justice, led by Bush-intimate Attorney General Alberto Gonzalez, will never bring such a case to the federal courts, but the United States Congress could lift sections of this well-researched case and use them as elements of articles of impeachment of George Bush, Dick Cheney, Donald Rumsfeld, and Condoleezza Rice.

"All impeachment would take is courage of members of Congress and a true love for our country, instead of loyalty to administration benefactors."

—ANN WRIGHT, retired U.S. Army Reserve Colonel (29 years) and U.S. diplomat who resigned in March 2003 in opposition to the war on Iraq

"Any American patriot who would like to see a grand jury challenge this Administration's blitzkrieg against our constitution will relish Elizabeth de la Vega's book *United States v. George W. Bush et al.* Machiavelli believed fraud was laudable and glorious in matters of war. In her book, Ms. de la Vega invites us into the courtroom to consider the indictment of our modern day Machiavellis and the fraud they've perpetrated."

—EDWARD ASNER

book makes the case. It shines a brilliant beam of light into the fog of ıstream news and politics. If you're tired of partisan rhetoric and media .sions, read *United States v. George W. Bush et al.*

"Elizabeth de la Vega puts you in the jury room—and gives you the evidence you need to decide whether Bush, Cheney, Rumsfeld, Rice, and Powell worked as a team to defraud the USA while dragging the country into the invasion of Iraq. Apologists for the war have tried to evade and deny the facts that can be found in *United States v. George W. Bush et al.* This meticulous book will make the evasions and denials more difficult."

—NORMAN SOLOMON, author of *War Made Easy: How Presidents and Pundits Keep Spinning Us to Death*

"In her truly engrossing study, former federal prosecutor Elizabeth de la Vega conducts a hypothetical but technically impeccable grand jury indictment of George Bush, Dick Cheney, Donald Rumsfeld, Condoleezza Rice, and Colin Powell for 'conspiracy to defraud the United States.' She marshals the evidence to show that they deliberately misinformed the people about the reasons for our war against Iraq. It is much more powerful than the 9/11 report. A *tour de force*."

—CHALMERS JOHNSON, author of *Blowback* and *The Sorrows of Empire*

"With her imaginative Grand Jury approach, Elizabeth de la Vega gives us a front-row seat for the evidence of violent crimes by high officials of the Bush administration. Her lively style and sense of humor pierce the all-too-familiar melancholy and make for a fascinating read. Give this book to friends who cannot get their head around the notion that our president lied us into an unnecessary war. But alert them to the possibility that they may be moved to act more responsibly than the frightened Germans of the 1930s and the apathetic neighbors of Kitty Genovese. For it will be clear that we are all in this together."

—RAY McGOVERN, retired CIA analyst

UNITED STATES
v.
GEORGE W. BUSH et al.

Elizabeth de la Vega
from TomDispatch.com

Seven Stories Press
New York / Toronto / London / Melbourne

A Seven Stories Press First Edition, published in association with TomDispatch.com.

Seven Stories Press
140 Watts Street
New York, NY 10013
http://www.sevenstories.com

In Canada:
Publishers Group Canada, 250A Carlton Street, Toronto, ON M5A 2L1

In the UK:
Turnaround Publisher Services Ltd., Unit 3, Olympia Trading Estate, Coburg Road, Wood Green, London N22 6TZ

In Australia:
Palgrave Macmillan, 627 Chapel Street, South Yarra, VIC 3141

Library of Congress Cataloging-in-Publication Data

De la Vega, Elizabeth.
United States v. George W. Bush et al. / Elizabeth de la Vega. -- 1st ed.
p. cm.
ISBN-13: 978-1-58322-756-5 (pbk. : alk. paper)
ISBN-10: 1-58322-756-3 (pbk. : alk. paper)
1. United States--Politics and government--2001- 2. Bush, George W. (George Walker), 1946- 3. Bush, George W. (George Walker), 1946---Friends and associates. 4. Iraq War, 2003---Political aspects. 5. Iraq War, 2003---Causes. 6. Misconduct in office--United States. 7. Political crimes and offenses--United States. 8. Fraud--Political aspects--United States. I. Title. II. Title: United States versus George W. Bush et al.

E902.D4 2006
973.931--dc22 2006028019

College professors may order examination copies of Seven Stories Press titles for a free six-month trial period. To order, visit www.sevenstories.com/textbook/, or fax on school letterhead to (212) 226-1411.

Book design by Jon Gilbert
Printed in Canada

9 8 7 6 5 4 3 2 1

For Paul, the best man I know

For Kathy, who taught me to shoot the moon

For Chris and Danny, I am so proud of you

CONTENTS

HELEN THOMAS: Ari, is the President willing to prepare to sacrifice American and Iraqi innocent lives to take out Saddam Hussein?

ARI FLEISCHER: Helen, the President is prepared to protect innocent lives.

HELEN THOMAS: Pardon?

ARI FLEISCHER: The President is prepared to protect innocent lives. And that is why the President has said that Iraq is part of the axis of evil.

September 3, 2002, White House Press Briefing by Ari Fleischer

INTRODUCTION

A FRAUD WORSE THAN ENRON

Elizabeth de la Vega, appearing on behalf of the United States. That is a phrase I've uttered hundreds of times in twenty years as a federal prosecutor. I retired two years ago. So, obviously, I do not now speak for any U.S. Attorney's Office, nor do I represent the federal government. This should be apparent from the fact that I am proposing a hypothetical indictment of the President and his senior advisers—not a smart move for any federal employee who wishes to remain employed. Lest anyone miss the import of this paragraph, let me emphasize that it is a DISCLAIMER: I am writing as a private citizen.

Obviously, as a private citizen, I cannot simply draft and file an indictment. Nor can I convene a grand jury. Instead, in the following pages I intend to present a hypothetical indictment to a hypothetical grand jury. The defendants are President George W. Bush, Vice President Richard Cheney, Secretary of Defense Donald Rumsfeld, Secretary of State Condoleezza Rice, and former Secretary of State Colin Powell. The crime is tricking the nation into war—in legal terms, conspiracy to defraud the United States. And all of you are invited to join the grand jury.

We will meet for seven days. On day one, I'll present the indictment in the morning and in the afternoon I will explain the applicable law. On days two through seven, we'll have witness testimony, presented in transcript form, with exhibits.

As is the practice in most grand jury presentations, the evidence will be presented in summary form, by federal agents—except that these agents are hypothetical. (Any relationship to actual federal agents, living or deceased, is purely coincidental.)

On day seven, when the testimony is complete, I'll leave the room to allow the grand jury to vote.

If the indictment and grand jury are hypothetical, the evidence is not. I've prepared for this case, just as I would have done for any other case in my years as a prosecutor, by reviewing all of the available relevant information. In this case, such information consists of witness accounts, the defendants' speeches, public remarks, White House press briefings, interviews, congressional testimony, official documents, all public intelligence reports, and various summaries of intelligence, such as in the reports of the Senate Select Committee on Intelligence and the 9/11 Commission. I've discarded any evidence, however compelling, that is uncorroborated.

Then, using a sophisticated system of documents piled on every surface in my dining room, I've organized and analyzed the reliable information chronologically, by topic, and by defendant. I've compared what the President and his advisers have said publicly to what they knew and said behind the scenes. Finally, I've presented the case through testimony that will, I hope, make sense and keep everybody awake.

After analyzing this evidence in light of the applicable

law, I've determined that we already have more than enough information to allow a reasonable person to conclude that the President conducted a wide-ranging effort to deceive the American people and Congress into supporting a war against Iraq. In other words, in legal terms, there is probable cause to believe that Bush, Cheney, Rumsfeld, Rice, and Powell violated Title 18, United States Code, Section 371, which prohibits conspiracies to defraud the United States. Probable cause is the standard of proof required for a grand jury to return an indictment. Consequently, we have more than sufficient evidence to warrant indictment of the President and his advisers.

Do I expect someone to promptly indict the President and his aides? No. I am aware of the political impediments and constitutional issues relating to the indictment of a sitting president. Do those impediments make this merely an empty exercise? Absolutely not.

I believe this presentation adds a singular perspective to the debate about the President's use of prewar intelligence: that of an experienced federal prosecutor. Certainly, scholars and experts such as Barbara Olshansky, David Lindorff, Michael Ratner, John Dean, and Elizabeth Holtzman have written brilliantly about the legal grounds for impeachment that arise from the President's misrepresentations about the grounds for an unprovoked invasion of Iraq. But for most Americans, the debate about White House officials' responsibility for false preinvasion statements remains fixed on, and polarized around, the wrong question: Did the President and his team lie about the grounds for war? For many, the suggestion that the

President lied is heresy, more shocking than a Baptist minister announcing during vespers that he's a cross-dresser. For many others—indeed, now the majority of Americans—that the President lied to get his war is a given, although no less shocking.

So my goals are threefold. First, I want to explain that under the law that governs charges of conspiracy to defraud, the legal question is not whether the President lied. The question is not whether the President subjectively believed there were weapons of mass destruction in Iraq. The legal question that must be answered is far more comprehensive: Did the President and his team defraud the country? After swearing to uphold the law of the land, did our highest government officials employ the universal techniques of fraudsters—deliberate concealment, misrepresentations, false pretenses, half-truths—to deceive Congress and the American people?

My second goal is to supplement the scholarly analyses already written, by moving beyond exposition, beyond theory, to the inside of the courtroom, or more precisely, the grand jury room. By presenting the President's conspiracy to defraud just as a prosecutor would present any fraud conspiracy, I hope to enable readers to consider the case in an uncharged atmosphere, applying criminal law to the evidence that they believe has been proved to the standard of probable cause, just as grand jurors would in any other case.

Why is it important to do this? Because whether the President and his senior officials conspired to defraud the United States about the grounds for war is, at least on one level, a legal question, but, without a shift in political will, there will never be any reasoned consideration of it as such. The President will not be held accountable for misrepresenting the prewar intelligence unless and until Congress conducts hearings similar to the Watergate hearings. As yet, however, we seem painfully incapable of reaching that point. We are like inept tennis partners, collectively letting the ball slip by in the no-man's-land between the service line and the baseline, or in this case, between the legal and the political.

Perhaps more important, however, is that, although the evidence of wrongdoing is overwhelming, the facts are so complicated—far more so than those that prompted the Watergate hearings—that it's impossible to have a productive debate about them in the political sphere. Indeed, modern-day spin has vanquished substance so thoroughly that even the most well-grounded charge of deliberate deception is often considered more despicable than the deception itself.

One forum where that's not true is the courtroom. The court system is far from perfect, but there we at least expect that people will not substitute personal attacks for argument. We expect a reasoned exploration of fact versus fiction, honest mistake versus deliberate fraud. We also expect, and the law requires, that people hear *all the evidence* before deciding, thereby avoiding the rapid volley of sound bites that so regularly masquerades for debate on television. Hence, this hypothetical grand jury presentation: it is a vehicle to deliver a message.

My third goal is to send the message home—to whomever will listen. And this is it:

The President has committed fraud.
It is a crime in the legal, not merely the colloquial, sense.
It is far worse than Enron.
It is not a victimless crime.
We cannot shrug our shoulders and walk away.

WHY? BECAUSE WE ARE ALL KITTY GENOVESE'S NEIGHBORS

As an Assistant U. S. Attorney in Minneapolis, a member of the Organized Crime Strike Force in San Jose, and Chief of the San Jose Branch U.S. Attorney's Office, I prosecuted all manner of criminal cases. There were bank embezzlements, government frauds, violent takeover robberies, piloting a commercial passenger flight while under the influence—the pilot had had twenty rum and (diet) Cokes and four hours' sleep before takeoff—and investment frauds, to name a few. Most were interesting; some downright loopy. One hapless fellow, for example, stole a truck filled with frozen turkeys and drove it across state lines to Wisconsin, thereby landing himself in federal prison rather than in county jail. For good measure, the following week—before he'd been apprehended for the frozen-turkey heist—he stole a truck filled with packaged frozen broccoli and drove it to Iowa.

Unquestionably, though, the most compelling cases were those that involved victims—of violent crimes, robberies, or fraud. So I was not surprised to hear the lead

Enron prosecutor's comment after the jury convicted former Enron CEOs Ken Lay and Jeffrey Skilling: "What inspired me," John Hueston said, "was just that, that I had spoken to so many employees, so many victims who lost their savings, people who pleaded with me and the other prosecutors to see justice done."

Thanks to Hueston and his team, the victims of the Enron fraud—a $68 billion dollar crime that left 20,000 people without jobs, pensions, and life's savings—have obtained some measure of justice. They will never be made whole, but at least the CEOs who orchestrated the fraud have been held accountable. In the case of the largest corporate fraud ever prosecuted in the United States, the system has worked, albeit imperfectly.

Thus far, however, in the case of the vastly broader and more devastating Iraq war fraud orchestrated by the CEO of the United States and his management team, the system has failed. And we are all victims of this fraud. George W. Bush exploited the vulnerability of an entire populace reeling from the September 11, 2001, attacks to manipulate them into supporting a war based on false pretenses. If the financial cost of the President's fraud is astronomical—$340 billion in direct war costs alone as of August 2006—the human cost is incalculable, and far more profound: over 2,500 American soldiers killed and 19,000 wounded; possibly many more than 50,000 Iraqis killed; untold numbers of grieving Iraqi and American family members; hundreds of thousands of Iraqis homeless; and a million soldiers who have been sent to this war and will never be the same.

While we are all victims of the President's crime, we are also all bystanders. The crime is ongoing, happening right before our eyes, and we are all onlookers; *we are all, in a sense, Kitty Genovese's neighbors.*

As Malcolm Gladwell recounts in his book *The Tipping Point*, Kitty Genovese was viciously assaulted, stabbed three times, and finally killed, on the way to her Queens, New York, home one night in 1964. Thirty-eight neighbors heard or watched her ordeal, but no one called the police until the attack was essentially over. The murder was universally seen as a horrifying example of modern-day indifference to the plight of others. But, Gladwell explains, psychologists Bibb Latane and John Darley conducted experiments that led to a far different explanation: "When people are in a group . . . responsibility for acting is diffused. They assume that someone else will make the call, or they assume that because no one else is acting, the apparent problem . . . is not really a problem." Ironically, then, it was not that no one called to help Kitty Genovese "*despite* the fact that thirty-eight people heard her scream; it's that no one called *because* thirty-eight people heard her scream."

For over a year now, polls have shown that the majority of Americans believe President Bush deliberately misrepresented prewar intelligence. Executive branch officials who deliberately mislead Congress and the public intending to influence congressional action have committed a federal crime. That means that roughly 100 million Americans believe Bush has committed a crime, yet most, like Kitty Genovese's neighbors, are just passive bystanders—although not, I believe, due to indifference.

Indeed, many of us are just watching it happen because we feel powerless to stop it. Hundreds of thousands of people *have*, in effect, called 911, but not even Democrats in Congress have been willing to answer the phone. It is not that they don't have enough information; it is, our Democratic representatives say, because it is not good political strategy.

The proposition that it is not good political strategy to insist that government officials obey the law is highly debatable. More important, strategizing in the face of an ongoing crime is wrong. Ask any legislator whether he would strategize about possible political fallout before intervening to stop a crime that was occurring in front of his eyes and the response would be, "Of course not." But that is exactly what's happening right now.

So, consider this my 911 call. I'm calling on Democrats *and* Republicans to do the right thing. And I'm calling on everyone else to do whatever you can to convince Congress to do the right thing. I am not talking about *bringing people to justice* in the vengeful sense that President Bush employs. I am talking about effecting justice. I am talking, finally, about holding our highest government officials accountable for a complex and calculated program of false pretense, misleading statements, and material omissions—a criminal betrayal of trust that is strikingly similar to, yet far worse than, the fraud committed by Enron's top officials.

ENRON: MISLEADING STATEMENTS AND MATERIAL OMISSIONS

In July of 2002, President Bush stood before a snappy blue-and-white banner marked "Corporate Responsibility" and announced that he was opposed to fraud. With the enactment of the new Corporate Corruption Act, the President declared, there would "not be a different ethical standard for corporate America than the standard that applies to everyone else. The honesty you expect in your small businesses, or in your workplace . . . will be expected and enforced in every corporate suite in this country." CEOs would now have to personally vouch for the truth of their public statements.

Bush's speech announcing a higher standard for CEOs was itself misleading. Hearing it, one might easily conclude that if the President hadn't pushed for this new law, corporate officers would be legally entitled to lie, cheat, and steal. Not true, of course. The new law, also called the Sarbanes-Oxley Act, did not suddenly, for the first time in United States history, require corporate officials to be truthful, forthright, and fair with the public. Such obligations have been inherent in criminal fraud and other statutes for years.

Indeed, the Enron prosecution did not involve the Sarbanes-Oxley Act at all. The main charge was conspiracy to defraud: that is, conspiring to deceive investors by manipulating financial data, making false and misleading statements, and deliberately omitting important facts, in violation of Title 18, United States Code, Section 371.

Manipulation of data, false and misleading statements, and material omissions—sound familiar?

At trial, former Enron CEOs Kenneth Lay and Jeffrey Skilling claimed they were not responsible for the deception because they had no idea what their underlings were doing. As the jury was instructed, however, anyone who makes representations intending that the public will rely on them, has an *affirmative obligation* to make sure that they are true and accurate. Representations made with reckless indifference to their truth are as false as outright lies.

After four months of complex testimony, the jury reached a simple conclusion: Lay and Skilling were responsible for what went on their company. As school principal Freddie Delgado put it: "I can't say that I don't know what my teachers were doing in the classroom. I am still responsible if a child gets lost."

In other words, the Enron jurors concluded that, legally, the desks of CEOs Lay and Skilling were the final repositories of the proverbial buck. Those jurors were average Americans—office workers, educators, engineers, a nurse—and they knew, even without the Sarbanes-Oxley Act, that CEOs should be held to the same standards of honesty and accountability that they would apply to themselves in their own lives. Faced with evidence that Lay and Skilling had repeatedly made public statements that were seriously undermined, if not flatly contradicted, by information and warnings they had received behind the scenes, the jury refused to allow them to avoid responsibility by blaming their subordinates.

IRAQ: MISLEADING STATEMENTS AND MATERIAL OMISSIONS

The techniques of deception used by George W. Bush and his aides are identical to those used by Lay and Skilling. In his July 2002 speech announcing the signing of the Corporate Corruption Bill, the President said, "The only fair risks are [those] based on honest information." The President and his top advisers were acutely aware of the solemn risks posed by an invasion of Iraq, but instead of debating those risks honestly, they developed slogans, including the familiar "risks of inaction are greater than the risks of action" that simultaneously usurped and deflected counterarguments while providing no information whatsoever, honest or otherwise.

Such propaganda, cynical and craven as it is, might not qualify as criminal fraud, but the propaganda alone was insufficient to convince Congress and the American people to invest in the plan for war. To remedy this deficiency and close the deal, the President and his top aides made hundreds of representations, both general and specific, that were carefully crafted to manipulate public opinion. As we now know, many of those assertions were false and misleading. More important, we also now know that President Bush and his advisers had notice and direct knowledge that their representations were seriously undermined and in some key instances, disproved by information that was available to them. Consistently, the President and his aides knowingly conveyed false impressions, concealed important information, made deliberate misrepresentations, and professed certainty about facts that were speculative at best. Such is the definition of criminal fraud—whether committed by the President of the United States or the CEO of a major corporation.

The only difference between the fraud committed by the Enron officers and the fraud committed by the President is that the latter was far more comprehensive and far more calculated. Even as President Bush stood center stage endorsing honesty that July four years ago, he and his company were setting the stage for another show. If the "only fair risks" speech was a perky Frank Capra clip, the White House's next production would be twenty-first-century H.G. Wells.

As of July 30, 2002, Bush had directed the creation of the White House Iraq Group, a public-relations operation whose sole purpose was to market the war. This team, collectively called WHIG, was cochaired by the President's closest aides and long-term political consultants, Senior Adviser Karl Rove—whom Bush has described as "the architect" of his 2004 reelection campaign—and former Counselor to the President Karen Hughes.

By July 30, 2002, the White House Iraq Group had already begun fabricating an ominous scenario that blurred together the September 11 tragedy, mushroom clouds rising over American cities, and terrorists releasing strains of smallpox, interspersed with the shadowy face of a mad Iraqi dictator spring-loaded to attack the United States. They were collecting props—anthrax vials and undated photos showing centrifuge components and unidentifiable buildings where something ominous might be happening, *but we can't afford to wait to find out*. They were writing the script: power phrases like "Grave and gathering danger" and "We can't afford to let the smoking gun be a mushroom cloud," designed less to inform than to inflame. And, finally, Rove, Hughes, and company were scheduling appearances for the President's War Council members that would begin just a month later, in early September 2002.

It was to be a bravura performance by the President, the Vice President, the Secretary of Defense, the Secretary of State, the National Security Adviser, and many supporting cast members. The production was so well done, in fact, that, like the radio audience terrified into hysteria by the infamous "War of the Worlds" broadcast of 1938, most of us were fooled. Admittedly, we resisted buying the duct tape and plastic sheeting; we may not have wrapped our heads in wet towels to ward off Martian gas like the 1938 radio audience. What happened, however, was much worse: because of Bush's fiction, we agreed to bomb people 8,000 miles away whose only "crime" was that they were oppressed by a violent and cruel dictator.

Undoubtedly, Americans were panicked by H. G. Wells's radio play in part because they were exhausted and nervous in those tough Depression years. But Orson Welles' breathless report of a Martian invasion was never *intended* to cause panic, nor was it ultimately harmful.

The President's elaborate production was, and still remains, an entirely different story. It was a deliberate effort to create a permanent state of fear in America. And to say it was harmful is like saying that it hurts to get hit by a Mack truck.

Federal sentencing guidelines recognize that one who defrauds a vulnerable victim, such as a salesman who falsely represents the curative benefits of an elixir to a cancer patient, has committed an even more serious crime than one who defrauds a person who is not so "particularly susceptible." The President knew that Americans were "particularly susceptible" in 2002. We were exhausted, and justifiably terrified, not only because of September 11 but also because of the anthrax murders and the random Washington, DC, sniper killings that coincided with the Bush-Cheney administration's push for war.

President Bush and his White House Iraq Group did not merely exploit this fear; they magnified it. Worse yet, the President was the very person upon whom the public relied to protect it from danger and, one would hope, from omnipresent fear itself. Having used the authority of the Oval Office to make people *more* afraid, having created an even darker backdrop of fear, our highest officials exploited that reliance and the trust they enjoyed by virtue of their positions to sell something they knew the American public would not otherwise have bought. It was as if the cancer victim's trusted personal physician had convinced him that his disease was more advanced than it really was, and then used the same fraudulently heightened fear to manipulate him into buying a bogus cure-all.

In the language of criminal law, the President and his senior advisers have abused a position of trust to defraud the most vulnerable of victims. How would such a case be presented for prosecution? I invite you into the grand jury room to observe:

Ladies and Gentlemen, tomorrow begins our presentation in the case of United States v. George W. Bush et al. *Please remember that you must decide the case based solely on the evidence that's presented and the applicable law, without regard to prejudice or sympathy. In other words, your politics, and any personal feelings you have toward the defendants—positive or negative—should have no bearing on your deliberations.*

I will begin by passing out the indictment, so don't forget your reading glasses . . .

UNITED STATES v. GEORGE W. BUSH et al.

Grand Jury Presentation

9:00 A.M.

ASSISTANT UNITED STATES ATTORNEY: Good morning, Ladies and Gentlemen. We're here today in the case of *United States* v. *George W. Bush et al.* In addition to President Bush, the defendants are Vice President Richard B. Cheney, former National Security Adviser Condoleezza Rice—who's now the Secretary of State, of course—Secretary of Defense Donald Rumsfeld, and former Secretary of State Colin Powell.

It's a one-count proposed indictment: Conspiracy to Defraud the United States in violation of Title 18, United States Code, Section 371. I'll explain the law that applies to the case this afternoon, but I'm going to hand out the indictment now, so you'll have some context for that explanation. Take as long as you need to read it, and then feel free to take your lunch break, but please leave your copy of the indictment with the foreperson. We'll meet back at one o'clock.

• • •

UNITED STATES DISTRICT COURT

UNITED STATES OF AMERICA,	)	Criminal No.
Plaintiff,	)	
	)	Conspiracy to Defraud
v.	)	the United States
	)	
GEORGE W. BUSH,	)	18 U.S.C. Section 371
RICHARD B. CHENEY,	)	
CONDOLEEZZA RICE,	)	
DONALD M. RUMSFELD, and	)	
COLIN POWELL,	)	
Defendants	)	

INDICTMENT

THE GRAND JURY CHARGES:

Introductory Allegations

At times relevant to this Indictment:

1. The primary law of the United States Federal Government was set forth in the U.S. Constitution ("Constitution"), which provides that the first branch of government is the Legislative Branch ("Congress"). Pursuant to Article I, Section 8, Congress has certain powers and obligations regarding oversight of foreign affairs, including the powers to: (1) declare war; (2) raise and support the armed forces; and (3) tax and spend for the common good.

2. Article II of the Constitution establishes the Executive Branch.

The Executive Power of the United States is vested in the President, who is also the Commander in Chief of the Armed Services.

3. Defendant **GEORGE W. BUSH ("BUSH")** has been employed as President of the United States since January 20, 2001. On that day, **BUSH** took a constitutionally mandated oath to faithfully execute the Office of President and to preserve, protect, and defend the Constitution. **BUSH** is also constitutionally obligated to take care that the laws be faithfully executed.

4. As Chief Executive, **BUSH** exercised authority, direction, and control over the entire Executive Branch, which includes the White House, the Office of the Vice President, the Departments of State, Defense, and others, and the National Security Council.

5. Defendant **RICHARD B. CHENEY** ("**CHENEY**") has been employed as Vice President of the United States since January 20, 2001.

6. Defendant **CONDOLEEZZA RICE ("RICE")** was employed as the National Security Adviser from January 2001 to January 2005, when she became Secretary of State, a position she holds as of the date of this indictment. As National Security Adviser, **RICE** exercised direction, control, and authority over the National Security Council, which coordinates various national security and foreign policy agencies, including the Departments of Defense and State.

7. Defendant **DONALD M. RUMSFELD ("RUMSFELD")** has been employed as Secretary of Defense since January 2001.

8. Defendant **COLIN M. POWELL ("POWELL")** was employed as Secretary of State from January 2001 through January of 2005.

9. Before assuming their offices, **CHENEY**, **RICE**, **RUMSFELD** and **POWELL** took an oath to preserve, protect, and defend the Constitution.

10. As employees of the Executive Branch, **BUSH**, **CHENEY**, **RICE**, **RUMSFELD**, and **POWELL** were governed by Executive Orders 12674 and 12731. These Orders provide that Executive Branch employees hold their positions as a public trust and that the American people have a right to expect that they will fulfill that trust in accordance with certain ethical standards and principles. These include abiding by the Constitution and laws of the United States, as well as not using their offices to further private goals and interests.

11. Pursuant to the Constitution, their oaths of office, their status as Executive Branch employees, and their presence in the United States, **BUSH, CHENEY, RICE, RUMSFELD,** and **POWELL**, and their subordinates and employees, are required to obey Title 18, United States Code, Section 371, which prohibits conspiracies to defraud the United States.

12. As used in Section 371, the term "to defraud the United States" means "to interfere with or obstruct one of its lawful government functions by deceit, craft, trickery, or at least by means that are dishonest." The term also means to "impair, obstruct, or defeat the lawful function of any department of government" by the use of "false or fraudulent pretenses or representations."

13. A "false" or "fraudulent" representation is one that is: (a) made with knowledge that it is untrue; (b) a half-truth; (c) made without a reasonable basis or with reckless indifference as to whether it is, in fact, true or false; or (d) literally true, but intentionally presented in a manner reasonably calculated to deceive a person of ordinary prudence and intelligence. The knowing concealment or omission of information that a reasonable person would consider important in deciding an issue also constitutes fraud.

14. Congress is a "department of the United States" within the meaning of Section 371. In addition, hearings regarding funding for mil-

itary action and authorization to use military force are "lawful functions" of Congress.

15. Accordingly, the presentation of information to Congress and the general public through deceit, craft, trickery, dishonest means, and fraudulent representations, including lies, half-truths, material omissions, and statements made with reckless indifference to their truth or falsity, while knowing and intending that such fraudulent representations would influence Congress' decisions regarding authorization to use military force and funding for military action, constitutes interfering with, obstructing, impairing, and defeating a lawful government function of a department of the United States within the meaning of Section 371.

The Conspiracy to Defraud the United States

16. Beginning on or about a date unknown, but no later than August of 2002, and continuing to the present, in the District of Columbia and elsewhere, the defendants,

GEORGE W. BUSH,
RICHARD B. CHENEY,
CONDOLEEZZA RICE,
DONALD M. RUMSFELD, and
COLIN M. POWELL,

and others known and unknown, did knowingly and intentionally conspire to defraud the United States by using deceit, craft, trickery, dishonest means, false and fraudulent representations, including ones made without a reasonable basis and with reckless indifference to their truth or falsity, and omitting to state material facts necessary to make their representations truthful, fair and accurate, while knowing and intending that their false and fraudulent representations would influence the public and the deliberations of Congress with regard to authorization of a preventive war against Iraq, thereby defeating, obstructing, impairing, and interfering with Congress' lawful functions of overseeing foreign affairs and making appropriations.

17. **The Early Months of the Bush-Cheney Administration**: Prior to January of 2001, **BUSH**, **CHENEY**, and **RUMSFELD** each demonstrated a predisposition to employ U.S. military force to invade the Middle East, including, specifically, to forcibly remove Saddam Hussein.

18. Since 1992, **CHENEY** has endorsed a "bold foreign policy" that includes using military force to "punish" or "threaten to punish" possible aggressors in order to protect the United States's access to Persian Gulf oil and to halt proliferation of weapons of mass destruction ("WMD"), a term that is customarily used to describe chemical, biological, and nuclear weapons.

19. On or about January 26, 1998, **RUMSFELD** and seven other future **BUSH-CHENEY** administration appointees signed a letter sent by a conservative policy institute named "Project for a New American Century" ("PNAC") to then President William Clinton, which called for U.S. military action to forcibly remove Saddam Hussein from power.

20. In January 1999, **BUSH** named **RICE** and her future Deputy National Security Adviser Stephen Hadley ("Hadley"), as his presidential-campaign foreign-policy advisers, along with future Deputy Secretary of Defense Paul Wolfowitz ("Wolfowitz") and four others who had publicly advocated forcibly removing Saddam Hussein.

21. On or before September 2000, 12 future **BUSH-CHENEY** administration appointees, including Wolfowitz, former Assistant to Vice President **CHENEY**, I. Lewis "Scooter" Libby, and Rumsfeld's long-term aide Stephen Cambone, participated in drafting "Rebuilding America's Defenses," a PNAC policy statement which asserted that the "need for a substantial American force presence in the Gulf transcends the issue of the regime of Saddam Hussein." PNAC acknowledged that its goals would take

a long time to achieve "absent some catastrophic and catalyzing event—like a new Pearl Harbor."

22. Once **BUSH** became the Republican candidate in the 2000 presidential election campaign, he and **CHENEY** informed the general public that they would be reluctant to use military force and did not believe that the United States should engage in "nation-building."

23. On and after January 20, 2001, **BUSH** and **CHENEY** caused to be appointed as senior foreign policy advisors and consultants, at least thirty-four persons who had publicly endorsed the PNAC principles of United States global preeminence and use of force to "punish" or "threaten to punish" emerging threats from weapons of mass destruction ("WMD") or impediments to United States access to oil in the Middle East. Of those appointees, eighteen had also publicly advocated forcibly removing Saddam Hussein.

24. In late December 2000, **BUSH** and **CHENEY** advised outgoing President William J. Clinton and others that, among potential foreign policy issues, **BUSH's** primary concern was Iraq.

25. On February 11, 2001, **BUSH** ordered the first airstrikes since 1998 to be conducted outside of the United Nations ("UN") agreed-upon No-Fly zones, to get Saddam Hussein's "attention."

26. **The Attacks of September 11, 2001**. On September 11, 2001, nineteen men hijacked four commercial airplanes. They crashed two planes into the World Trade Towers in New York City and another into the Pentagon in Washington, DC. The fourth plane crashed in Pennsylvania. In total, nearly 3,000 people died as a result of the September 11, 2001, attacks ("9/11").

27. Shortly afterward, United States intelligence agencies determined that 9/11 was the work of the terrorist organization al Qaeda, spearheaded by Osama Bin Laden. Fifteen of the nineteen hijackers were from

Saudi Arabia, two from Yemen, and two from Lebanon. This information, along with the conclusion that no evidence linked the attacks to Saddam Hussein or al Qaeda, was immediately communicated to **BUSH**, **CHENEY**, **RICE**, **RUMSFELD**, **POWELL**, and others.

28. **BUSH-CHENEY** administration members began discussing an invasion of Iraq immediately after 9/11. **BUSH, RUMSFELD** and others also assigned various subordinates, including former counterterrorism czar Richard Clarke, CIA Director George Tenet, and General Richard Meyers to look for intelligence that could justify attacking Saddam Hussein's regime.

29. On September 17, 2001, **BUSH** secretly ordered the formulation of preliminary plans for an invasion of Iraq, while admitting to his aides that no evidence existed to justify an attack.

30. On or about September 18, 2001, in response to **BUSH**'s request, Clarke sent **RICE** a memo that stated: (a) the case for linking Hussein to 9/11 was weak; (b) only anecdotal evidence linked Hussein to al Qaeda; (c) Osama Bin Laden resented the secularism of Saddam Hussein; and (d) there was no confirmed reporting of Saddam cooperating with Bin Laden on unconventional weapons.

31. On September 20, 2001, **BUSH** informed British Prime Minister Tony Blair that after Afghanistan, the United States and Britain should return to the issue of invading Iraq.

32. **U.S. Intelligence Community Assessments of Risk from Iraq in Effect on November 2001**. On occasion, Executive Branch officials request assessments of current intelligence on risks posed by WMD in a given country. Although such assessments are coordinated by the Central Intelligence Agency ("CIA"), the final product incorporates the analyses, including dissenting opinions, of the intelligence branches of the Departments of State, Energy, Defense, the National Security Agency, and others, which are collectively called the Intelligence Community ("IC").

33. As of November 2001, the most recent assessment on Iraq was a December 2000 classified Intelligence Community Assessment ("ICA") called "Iraq: Steadily Pursuing WMD Capabilities." This ICA was a comprehensive update on possible Iraqi efforts to rebuild WMD and weapons delivery systems after the 1998 departure of International Atomic Energy Agency ("IAEA") representatives and UN weapons inspectors, who are collectively referred to as the United Nations Special Commission ("UNSCOM").

34. Regarding Iraq's possible nuclear program, the December 2000 NIE unanimously concluded that:

(a) The IAEA and UNSCOM had destroyed or neutralized Iraq's nuclear infrastructure, but Iraq still had a foundation for future nuclear reconstitution;
(b) Iraq was continuing low-level theoretical research and training, and attempting to obtain dual-use items that cold be used to reconstitute its nuclear program;
(c) if Iraq acquired a significant quantity of fissile material through foreign assistance, it could have a crude nuclear weapon within a year; if Iraq received foreign assistance, it would take five to seven years to produce enough weapons-grade fissile material for a nuclear weapon; and
(d) Iraq did not appear to have reconstituted its nuclear weapons program.

35. **Escalation of Military Activity and Planning for Invasion of Iraq.** On November 21, 2001, **BUSH** secretly ordered preparation of a formal war plan for invading Iraq. Thereafter, for sixteen months, the **BUSH-CHENEY** administration expended substantial U.S. government funds in military activity and planning for invasion of Iraq, all without notice to, or approval by, the U.S. Congress.

36. **BUSH** did not receive an extensive briefing about possible WMD in Iraq before ordering a war plan, nor did he discuss the legitimacy of grounds for war with anyone. **BUSH** received no such briefing until December 21, 2002.

37. On or about November 27, 2001, **RUMSFELD** asked General "Tommy" Franks, head of Central Command, which supervises Middle East operations, to immediately prepare an Iraq war plan in response to **BUSH**'s order.

38. Thereafter, Franks discussed numerous revised Iraq war plans with **RUMSFELD**. Between December 2001 and August 2002, **BUSH, CHENEY**, **RICE, RUMSFELD, POWELL**, and others held at least five lengthy meetings about Franks' plans. In August, **BUSH** ordered Franks to prepare to invade Iraq using the "Hybrid Plan," a combination of the "Running Start" and "Generated Start" plans developed previously.

39. During 2002, the United States and Great Britain increased air strikes in order to degrade Iraqi air defenses and began deploying troops to areas around Iraq.

40. On or about July 30, 2002, without approval by, or notice to, Congress, **BUSH** caused the diversion of $700 million from Afghanistan war funds into Iraq invasion preparations.

41. On September 5, 2002, without approval by, or notice to, Congress, **BUSH** caused approximately 100 United States and British aircraft to launch ballistic missiles at Iraq's major western air-defense facility.

42. By September 12, 2002, without approval by, or notice to, Congress, **BUSH** had caused the movement of 40,000 military personnel and over 350,000 tons of equipment to areas around Iraq. Franks also ordered Central Command to be moved to Al Udeid Air Base near Doha, Qatar.

43. **Behind-the-Scenes Strategizing with British Officials:** On or before March 2002, **BUSH, RICE**, Wolfowitz, and others secretly began discussing ways to persuade the public and foreign allies to accept Bush's goal of invading Iraq, with British Prime Minister Tony Blair ("Blair") and his advisers.

44. On March 12, 2002, in Washington, DC, **RICE** met with Blair's Foreign Policy Adviser Sir David Manning and informed him of **BUSH**'s problems with persuading "international opinion that military action against Iraq was necessary and justified."

45. On March 17, 2002, in Washington, DC, British Ambassador Sir Christopher Meyer advised Wolfowitz that the two countries should "wrongfoot" Saddam Hussein by seeking a UN resolution that would require the readmission of weapons inspectors with the expectation that Saddam would create a justification for war by obstructing the inspections.

46. On April 6, 2002, in Crawford, Texas, **BUSH** and Blair discussed strategies to sway public opinion regarding military action in Iraq. Blair agreed to support a United States invasion if the two countries obtained a UN resolution first.

47. In mid-July, 2002, in Washington, DC, White House officials discussed Iraq with visiting British officials. Upon their return to London, these officials reported the talks to Blair in a meeting at 10 Downing St. on July 23, 2002. Among other things, Blair's advisers suggested that he urge **BUSH** to devise a more realistic political strategy for attacking Iraq, because a desire for "regime change" would not justify military action under international law.

48. In mid-July, 2002, in Washington, DC, CIA Director Tenet and others talked about the Bush administration's intentions regarding Iraq with Sir Richard Dearlove, the head of British Intelligence.

49. On July 23, 2002, during the Downing St. meeting described above, Dearlove informed Blair that in the United States "Military action was now seen as inevitable. **BUSH** wanted to remove Saddam, through military action, justified by the conjunction of terrorism and WMD. But the intelligence and facts were being fixed around the policy."

50. On July 23, 2002, British Foreign Secretary Jack Straw also noted that **BUSH** had "made up his mind to take military action." Straw said he would urge **POWELL** to persuade **BUSH** to seek a UN resolution requiring Saddam Hussein to readmit weapons inspectors, in effect, suggesting the "wrongfooting" strategy that Meyer had described to Wolfowitz.

51. **Behind-the-Scenes Efforts to Fix Intelligence Around the Policy.** Within weeks after learning from Clarke, Tenet, and others that Iraq and Saddam Hussein had no involvement with either 9/11 or al Qaeda, **RUMSFELD** caused Deputy Undersecretary for Defense Douglas Feith ("Feith") to secretly create the Counter Terrorism Group ("CTEG"), a small unit of political appointees whose mission was to find links between Iraq and al Qaeda by reviewing raw intelligence that previously had been discarded as unreliable. CTEG reported weekly to **RUMSFELD**'s long-term associate Stephen Cambone, and occasionally presented information directly to Wolfowitz, thereby circumventing standard IC procedures.

52. At some time in 2002, Feith also designated political appointees to work under his supervision in the newly-created Office of Special Plans, whose purpose was to develop and package information for use in marketing the President's plan for an invasion of Iraq. In the fall of 2002, this group presented information directly to **RUMSFELD**, to **RICE**'s office, and to **CHENEY**'s office, thereby circumventing standard IC procedures.

53. In the spring of 2002, **CHENEY** and his former aide, I. Lewis "Scooter" Libby, began visiting CIA headquarters to question CIA agents' assessments about Iraq. **RUMSFELD** and Deputy National

Security Adviser Hadley also repeatedly pressed CIA Director Tenet and his subordinates to present a stronger case against Iraq.

54. **Bush's Creation of the White House Iraq Group.** By the summer of 2002, domestic and international support for **BUSH'**s plan to invade Iraq was lukewarm. At the same time, Bush's chief political strategist and Senior Adviser Karl Rove and Kenneth Mehlman, head of the White House Office of Strategic Initiatives, were beginning to coordinate the President's involvement in the November 7, 2002, congressional election. Their overall goal was to gain Republican majorities in both houses of Congress so that the President would have the greatest possible support for his policies. Rove had specifically recommended that Republicans "focus on war" as a way to win elections. Consequently, in the summer of 2002, **BUSH**'s efforts to win support for an invasion of Iraq and his efforts to assist Republican congressional candidates became inextricably intertwined.

55. In the summer of 2002, **BUSH** caused the creation of the White House Iraq Group, which was cochaired by **BUSH**'s long-term political operatives Karl Rove and Karen Hughes, who remained **BUSH**'s close associate even though she had resigned her position as Counselor to the President. This team, also called WHIG, was largely a political and public-relations entity that included **RICE,** Hadley, President's Chief of Staff Andrew Card, President's legislative liaison Nicholas Calio, **CHENEY**'s key aide and veteran Republican political strategist Mary Matalin, **CHENEY**'s senior adviser Libby, and James Wilkinson, another Republican campaign consultant.

56. On or about September 6, 2002, Rove and Card publicly announced that: (a) the **BUSH-CHENEY** administration was beginning to "roll out" its case for an invasion of Iraq; (b) its public-relations campaign was specifically directed at forcing Congress to pass a resolution authorizing the President to use military force in Iraq; (c) **BUSH** wanted the resolution passed in about five weeks, before the 2002 election; and (d) in the end, it would be difficult for any legislator to vote against it.

57. **The Defendants' Massive Fraud to "Market" an invasion of Iraq**. On or about September 4, 2002, **BUSH** staged a photo opportunity with a bipartisan group of congressional leaders, after which he falsely and fraudulently announced that Iraq posed a serious threat to the safety of the United States and the world, while concealing from Congress and the American people the material facts that: (a) he had no reasonable basis whatsoever for his assertion; (b) he had never discussed the legitimacy of the grounds for an attack against Iraq with anyone; (c) he had never extensively reviewed existing intelligence regarding any possible threat from Iraq; (d) he had not requested an updated intelligence assessment on Iraq; (e) the United States intelligence assessment then in effect stated that Iraq had neither nuclear weapons nor a nuclear weapons program; and (f) the IC had consistently reported that Iraq had no involvement in 9/11 and no relationship with al Qaeda.

58. On September 4, 2002, **BUSH** also falsely and fraudulently claimed he was beginning an "open dialogue" with the American public, with Congress, and with United States allies to decide how to respond to Iraq, while concealing the material facts that he: (a) had requested a formal plan to invade Iraq nearly a year before; (b) had been conducting significant military and nonmilitary planning and attacks against Iraq for a year; (c) had directed significant military deployment to areas around Iraq; (d) was planning a massive air assault against Iraq's air defense facility for the next day; and (e) intended to work with the UN only to create a justification to use military force against Iraq.

59. Thereafter, the defendants and WHIG executed a calculated and wide-ranging strategy to deceive Congress and the American people by making hundreds of false and fraudulent representations that were only half-true, or literally true but misleading; by concealing material facts; and by making statements without a reasonable basis and with reckless indifference to their truth, regarding, among other things:

(a) their true intent to invade Iraq;
(b) the extent of military buildup and force used against Iraq without notice to or approval by Congress;
(c) their true purpose in seeking a Congressional resolution authorizing the use of military force against Iraq;
(d) their true intent to use their involvement in seeking a UN resolution requiring Iraq to cooperate with weapons inspectors as a sham; and
(e) their claimed justifications for invading Iraq, including but not limited to:

- The alleged connection between Saddam Hussein and the attacks of September 11, 2001;
- The alleged connection between Iraq and al Qaeda;
- The alleged connection between Saddam Hussein and any terrorists whose primary animus was directed towards the United States;
- Saddam Hussein's alleged intent to attack the United States in any way;
- Saddam Hussein's possession of nuclear weapons and the status of any alleged ongoing nuclear weapons programs;
- The lack of any reasonable basis for asserting with certainty that Saddam Hussein was actively manufacturing chemical and biological weapons; and
- The alleged urgency of any threat posed to the United States by Saddam Hussein.

60. **Congressional Joint Resolution to Authorize Use of Force Against Iraq.** As a result of the defendants' false and fraudulent "marketing" of the President's plan to invade Iraq, on October 11, 2002, the U.S Congress, acting pursuant to its Article I constitutional authority to oversee and authorize use of military force, passed a Congressional Joint Resolution to Authorize Use of Force Against Iraq ["the Resolution"] which stated:

> The President is authorized to use the Armed Forces of the United States as he determines to be necessary and appropriate in order to—
> (a) defend the national security of the United States against the continuing threat posed by Iraq; and
> (b) enforce all relevant United Nations Security Council resolutions regarding Iraq.

61. The Resolution required the President to, either before or within 48 hours after exercising the authority to use force, make available to the Senate and the House of Representatives his determination that:

> (a) reliance by the United States on further diplomatic or other peaceful means alone either (1) will not adequately protect the national security of the United States against the continuing threat posed by Iraq or (2) is not likely to lead to enforcement of all relevant United Nations Security Council resolutions regarding Iraq; and
>
> (b) acting pursuant to this resolution is consistent with the United States and other countries continuing to take the necessary actions against international terrorists and terrorist organizations, including those nations, organizations or persons who planned, authorized, committed or aided the terrorists attacks that occurred on September 11, 2001.

62. The Resolution also required the President to, at least every 60 days, present Congress a report on "matters relevant to this joint resolution."

63. In furtherance of the above-described conspiracy, the defendants and their coconspirators committed and caused to be committed the following overt acts:

Overt Acts

A. On December 9, 2001, **CHENEY** announced on NBC's *Meet the Press* that "it was pretty well confirmed" that lead 9/11 hijacker Mohamed Atta had met the head of Iraqi intelligence in Prague in April 2001, which statement was, as **CHENEY** well knew, made without reasonable basis and with reckless disregard for the truth, because it was based on a single witness's uncorroborated allegation that had not been fully investigated by U.S. intelligence agencies.

B. On July 15, 2002, **POWELL** stated on Ted Koppel's *Nightline*: "What we have consistently said is that the President has no plan on his desk to invade Iraq at the moment, nor has one been presented to him, nor have his advisors come together to put a plan to him," which statement was deliberately false and misleading in that it deceitfully implied the President was not planning an invasion of Iraq when, as **POWELL** well knew, the President was close to finalizing detailed military plans for such an invasion that he had ordered months previously.

C. On August 26, 2002, **CHENEY** made numerous false and fraudulent statements including: "Simply stated there is no doubt that Saddam Hussein now has weapons of mass destruction. There is no doubt that he is amassing them to use against our friends, against our allies, and against us," when, as **CHENEY** well knew, this statement was made without reasonable basis and with reckless indifference to the truth in that the IC's then prevailing assessment was that Iraq had neither nuclear weapons nor a reconstituted nuclear weapons program.

D. On September 7, 2002, appearing publicly with Blair, **BUSH** claimed a recent IAEA report stated that Iraq was "six months away from developing a [nuclear] weapon" and "I don't know what more evidence we need," which statements were made without basis and with reckless indifference to the truth in that: (1) the IAEA had not even been present in Iraq since 1998; and (2) the report the IAEA did write in 1998 had concluded there was no indication that Iraq had the physical capacity to produce weapons-usable nuclear material or that it had attempted to obtain such material.

E. On September 8, 2002, on *Late Edition with Wolf Blitzer,* **RICE** asserted that Saddam Hussein was acquiring aluminum tubes that were "only suited" for nuclear centrifuge use, which statement was deliberately false and fraudulent, and made with reckless indifference to the truth in that it omitted to state the following material facts: (1) the U.S. intelligence community was deeply divided about the likely use of the tubes; (2) there were at least fifteen intelligence reports written since April 2001 that cast doubt on the tubes' possible nuclear-related use; and (3) the U.S. Department of Energy nuclear weapons experts had concluded, after analyzing the tubes's specifications and the circumstances of the Iraqis' attempts to procure them, that the aluminum tubes were not well suited for nuclear centrifuge use and were more likely intended for artillery rocket production.

F. On September 8, 2002, **RUMSFELD** stated on *Face the Nation*: "Imagine a September 11th, with weapons of mass destruction. It's not three thousand, it's tens of thousands of innocent men, women and children," which statement was deliberately fraudulent and misleading in that it implied without reasonable basis and in direct contradiction to then prevailing intelligence that Saddam Hussein had no operational relationship with al Qaeda and was unlikely to provide weapons to terrorists.

G. On September 19, 2002, **RUMSFELD** told the Senate Armed Services Committee that "no terrorist state poses a greater or more immediate threat to the security of our people than the regime of Saddam Hussein," which statement was, as Rumsfeld well knew, made without reasonable basis and with reckless indifference to the truth in that: (1) Hussein had not acted aggressively toward the United States since his alleged attempt to assassinate President George H. W. Bush in 1993; (2) Iraq's military forces and equipment were severely debilitated because of

UN sanctions imposed after the 1991 Gulf War; (3) the IC's opinion was that Iraq's sponsorship of terrorists was limited to ones whose hostility was directed toward Israel; and (4) Iran, not Iraq, was the most active state sponsor of terrorism.

H. On October 1, 2002, the defendants caused the IC's updated classified National Intelligence Estimate to be delivered to Congress just hours before the beginning of debate on the Authorization to Use Military Force. At the same time, the defendants caused an unclassified "White Paper" to be published which was false and misleading in many respects in that it failed to include qualifying language and dissents that substantially weakened their argument that Iraq posed a serious threat to the United States.

I. On October 7, 2002, in Cincinnati, Ohio, **BUSH** made numerous deliberately misleading statements to the nation, including stating that in comparison to Iran and North Korea, Iraq posed a uniquely serious threat, which statement **BUSH** well knew was false and fraudulent in that it omitted to state the material fact that a State Department representative had been informed just three days previously that North Korea had actually already produced nuclear weapons. The defendants continued to conceal this information until after Congress passed the Authorization to Use Military Force against Iraq.

J. Between September 1, 2002, and November 2, 2002, **BUSH** traveled the country making in excess of thirty congressional-campaign speeches in which he falsely and fraudulently asserted that Iraq was a "serious threat" which required immediate action, when as he well knew, this assertion was made without reasonable basis and with reckless indifference to the truth.

K. In his January 28, 2003 State of the Union address, **BUSH** announced that the "British have recently learned that Iraq was seeking significant quantities of uranium from Africa" which statement was fraudulent and misleading and made with reckless disregard for the truth, in that it falsely implied that the information was true, when the CIA had advised the administration more than once that the allegation was unsupported by available intelligence.

L. In a February 5, 2003, speech to the UN, **POWELL** falsely implied, without reasonable basis and with reckless disregard for the truth, that, among other things: (1) those who maintained that Iraq was purchasing aluminum tubes for rockets were allied with Saddam Hussein, even though **POWELL** well knew that both Department of Energy nuclear weapons experts and State Department intelligence analysts had concluded that the tubes were not suited for nuclear centrifuge use; and (2) Iraq had an ongoing cooperative relationship with al Qaeda, when he well knew that no intelligence agency had reached that conclusion.

M. On March 18, 2003, **BUSH** sent a letter to the Speaker of the House of Representatives and the President Pro Tempore of the Senate which asserted that further reliance on diplomatic and peaceful means alone would not either: (1) adequately protect United States national security against the "continuing threat posed by Iraq" or (2) likely lead to enforcement of all relevant UN Security Council resolutions regarding Iraq, which statement was made without reasonable basis and with reckless indifference to the truth in that, as **BUSH** well knew, the U.S. intelligence community had never reported that Iraq posed an urgent threat to the United States and there was no evidence whatsoever to prove that Iraq had either the means or intent to attack the U.S. directly or indirectly. The statement was also false because, as **BUSH** well knew, the UN weapons inspectors had not found any weapons of mass destruction in Iraq and wanted to continue the inspection process because it was working well.

N. In the same March 18, 2003, letter, **BUSH** also represented that taking action pursuant to the Resolution was "consistent with continuing to take the necessary actions against international terrorists and terrorist organizations, including those nations, organizations or persons who planned, authorized, committed, or aided the terrorists attacks that occurred on

September 11, 2001," which statement was entirely false and without reasonable basis in that, as **BUSH** well knew, Iraq had no involvement with al Qaeda or the terrorist attacks of September 11, 2001.

All in violation of Title 18, United States Code, Section 371.

A TRUE BILL

Dated:

____

Foreperson

End of Indictment

• • •

1:00 P.M.

ASSISTANT U.S. ATTORNEY: All twenty-four of you are back, I see, so we're ready to go. Did everyone have enough time to read the indictment?

GRAND JUROR: We did, but could we get some heat in here? It's freezing.

SECOND GRAND JUROR: No it's not.

GRAND JUROR: Yes it is.

ASSISTANT U.S. ATTORNEY: Well, this does not bode well for your deliberations . . . Actually, I think it's chilly too, but for some perverse reason, the General Services Administration decides to turn on the heat only around Memorial Day. Then, around Halloween, they crank up the air conditioning. I'll see what I can do, but GSA is essentially a fourth branch of government . . .

Speaking of which—today we're going to discuss the law that applies to *U.S.* v. *Bush et al.* As you've just read, the indictment alleges a violation of the federal conspiracy statute, Title 18, United States Code, Section 371. Criminals have the option of violating Section 371 in one of two ways. They may conspire to violate another statute, such as bank robbery or kidnapping, or they may conspire "to defraud the United States, or an agency thereof," which is what's charged in this indictment. To understand conspiracy to defraud the United States, we need to address three main concepts:

1. What is a conspiracy?
2. What does it mean "to defraud the United States"?
3. What is fraud, generally?

What does conspiracy mean in the legal sense? This probably does not come as a surprise, but words do not necessarily have the same meaning in the legal sense that they have in everyday usage. Take the word "conspiracy," for example. Somehow, the word conspiracy has gotten a bad name. Everybody hears it and thinks, *oooh*, secret handshakes and people in trench coats talking into their sleeves.

GRAND JUROR: Does *oooh* have a specific legal meaning?

ASSISTANT U.S. ATTORNEY: I'll have to look that up. Anyway, criminal defense attorneys like to capitalize on this common connotation, which is exactly what happened in the recent trial of Enron CEOs Jeffrey Skilling and Ken Lay. Enron, as you know, is the Texas corporation that went belly up in the fall of 2001. Lay—who has now passed away—and Skilling were convicted of conspiracy to commit wire and securities fraud, among other things.

During the trial, the defense attorneys repeatedly referred to the conspiracy charge as the "giant conspiracy" or the "massive criminal conspiracy to cause the collapse of Enron." And, as prosecutor Katherine Ruemmler pointed out, it was always "in this mocking tone like it defies belief that there could have been a conspiracy at Enron." The defense attorneys were doing their jobs, trying to imply that the case was just plain ridiculous, but as they and Ruemmler—and the judge—knew, the term "conspiracy" has an entirely neutral meaning. It simply means "an agreement between two or more persons to join together to accomplish some unlawful purpose."

You don't have to be in a dingy basement or smoky hideaway to devise a conspiracy. On the contrary, most sophisticated conspiracies are planned and carried out by well-dressed executives in well-appointed offices.

Now, you may be wondering what legal rules from the Enron trial have to do with this case. The answer to that question requires a brief—really brief—law-school lesson. One source of criminal law, in addition to the statutes themselves, is what's called case law. Those are the opinions that judges publish on general legal principles and the proper interpretations of statutes in the context of specific court cases. Judges and scholars review this body of law and write pattern jury instructions for courts to use in advising trial juries.

So concepts that apply to one criminal case will apply to another, and it's worked that way for years. That is particularly true for conspiracy law, which we imported from England—along with scones—about 700 years ago, give or take a decade. I might use some examples from the Enron case, but the legal principles I'll be explaining are based on the pattern instructions.

How do you prove a conspiracy? Believe it or not, criminal conspiracies—and many crimes, actually—are almost always proved through circumstantial evidence, which is perfectly acceptable under the law. The term "circumstantial evidence" is the Rodney Dangerfield of legal terms. You often hear people say, *oh that's just a circumstantial case*, suggesting the evidence is flimsy, but, you may be surprised to hear, that is not at all how the law views direct and circumstantial evidence. On the contrary, juries are specifically instructed that the two are indistinguishable in terms of their importance.

When you know what direct and circumstantial evidence are, I think you'll see why this is true. Direct evidence is proof of a firsthand observation, like seeing, smelling, touching, hearing. For example, if your cousin walks into your house and tells you it's raining, that would be *direct* evidence that it's raining.

If, on the other hand, your cousin comes running into your house wearing a mud-splattered yellow slicker and galoshes—if anyone even *wears* galoshes anymore—and drops a dripping umbrella on the floor, from that you could conclude that it's raining outside. That's circumstantial evidence, a chain of facts that indirectly proves another fact.

The truth is, circumstantial evidence is often more reliable and believable than direct evidence. If it's clear and sunny, for example, and your cousin walks in, perfectly dry, and says, "Wow, it's pouring out there," his statement is not going to seem particularly reliable, even though it is direct evidence.

What it comes down to is common sense. And common sense will tell you that, in real life, people don't write out agreements to commit crimes, or say, "Hey, everyone, let's start a conspiracy." That is why another standard jury instruction is that proof of a conspiracy does not require evidence that the defendants explicitly discussed details of the scheme or made some formal agreement.

A similar point is that, in most conspiracy cases—including this one—there is rarely a smoking gun or an insider who can lay out all the evidence. You decide what facts have been proved and then decide what inferences to draw from them. Here is what juries are told about that point: "You are permitted to draw such reasonable inferences from the testimony and exhibits as you feel are justified in the light of common experience." Just like you do, quite naturally, every day.

So, a conspiracy is an agreement. As applied to this case, it would be proved by showing a chain of circumstances—public statements and conduct, versus behind-the-scenes knowledge and discussion—that would lead a reasonable person to conclude that the defendants had, by their actions, demonstrated that they had agreed to defraud the United States.

What does it mean, "to defraud the United States?"

Courts have said that "to defraud the United States" means to use fraud to "interfere with, impair, obstruct or defeat lawful government functions of an agency or branch" of the United States, and of course, Congress's deliberations about war, making appropriations, and oversight of foreign affairs, are "lawful government functions of a branch of the United States." These are the duties and responsibilities assigned to them in Article I of the U.S. Constitution. Keep in mind, however, that the conspiracy to defraud does not have to succeed, so legally it is irrelevant whether any member of Congress was actually deceived. Although I think the evidence will show that they were. The focus is on whether the defendants used fraudulent means interfere with Congress's lawful functions.

Finally, what is fraud?

You know, analyzing a case in light of a statute is like taking apart one of those Russian nesting dolls—

GRAND JUROR: Matryoshka!

ASSISTANT U.S. ATTORNEY: Bless you.

GRAND JUROR: No, that's what they're called: Matryoshka.

ASSISTANT U.S. ATTORNEY: Oh, thanks. I thought you had allergies or something. Anyway, you break the statute down into clauses, then phrases, and then words. After you've taken it apart and know what the parts mean, you put it back together.

In the context of Section 371, the Supreme Court has said that fraud includes deceit, craft, trickery and dishonest means. Let me explain that.

First of all—and I have no idea why I am into Russian references today—

GRAND JUROR: Because it's like *Siberia* in here.

ASSISTANT U.S. ATTORNEY: I'm so sorry . . . Well, remember how the Russian novelist Leo Tolstoy once wrote, "Happy families are all alike"? The same is true of fraud. Regardless of whether you're talking about legitimate activities that become frauds or schemes that start out that way—like lottery scams—fraud cases are all alike. Things people can defraud others *about* are unlimited, but the *techniques* people use to defraud are remarkably consistent.

Now, remember that we're talking about fraud, not lying. You may have heard the comment, *To say that President Bush lied about prewar intelligence is a lie*. You'll have a chance to evaluate that, but whether Bush et al. committed a crime in misrepresenting the prewar intelligence on Iraq is not a question of lying; it's a question of whether they committed fraud.

Fraud includes lying, but it's much more than lying.

And a "scheme to defraud" is any plan or course of action that's intended to deceive another through false pretenses, representations, or promises.

Legally, a lie is by definition intentional: It's a statement made with knowledge that it's untrue and with intent to deceive. On that issue, a key point to be aware of is the concept of notice. *Continuing to assert something as true, even after receiving notice that would cause a reasonable person to inquire further about whether his statement is in fact true, is the same as knowingly and intentionally making a false statement.* The law provides that once a person has reason to doubt the accuracy or veracity of what he's saying, he can't just stick his head in the sand and later claim he made a good faith mistake.

GRAND JUROR: I don't get it.

ASSISTANT U.S. ATTORNEY: Well, for example, in the Enron case, the evidence showed that numerous people, including Sherron Watkins, a company accountant, warned Ken Lay that the company's accounting practices were suspicious. So he was on notice. Therefore, when he continued to say, as a matter of certainty, that Enron's financial condition was hunky-dory, he was knowingly making a false representation, especially when he had access to any company information he wanted to see.

You may find the same willful blindness in this case. For example, the evidence will show, I believe, that White House officials had notice, particularly from Energy Department experts, that should have led them to question, to say the least, their many assertions that Iraq was buying aluminum tubes for use in nuclear centrifuges.

Therefore, they had a legal duty to inquire further. Politicians may be able to effectively use "plausible deniability" as a defense, but criminal defendants can not.

Okay. Where were we? Lying and fraud. The two terms are not legally synonymous. There is a good reason for this, which we know from daily life. Just about everyone, at one point or another, has been snookered.

GRAND JUROR: Snockered?

ASSISTANT U.S. ATTORNEY: Not snockered—snookered—you know, tricked, by a salesperson or an advertisement. But rarely because of an outright lie. Outright lies are a lousy way to deceive people.

For example: Say—it's farfetched, I know—but say that, as a teenager, you went drinking in the woods with your friends after work one night. The next day your mother asks you where you were the night before. If you're normal, you do not say, "I was out drinking." But if you're smart, you don't tell an outright lie, such as "I was at Fred's house all night." Why? Because it's way too easy to disprove.

More likely, you tell a half-truth, like "Oh, I was just hanging out with Fred or Sally," conveniently skipping the *in the woods drinking* part. Your mother's ability to figure that part out would depend on her cross-examination skills.

The law of fraud is premised on a societal determination that we should not have to cross-examine those who make representations to the public intending to influence our important decisions. That is especially true with government officials, not only because they hold positions of public trust, but also because the average citizen has few, if any, ways to question their claims.

The bottom line is that proof of fraud does not require evidence of outright lies. Lies are simply a subset of fraud. A good way to think about it is this:

[Whereupon the Assistant U.S. Attorney draws a large circle on the board]

Remember Venn diagrams? In this rudimentary—

GRAND JUROR: I'll say.

ASSISTANT U.S. ATTORNEY: Well, that's very hurtful . . . But you do recognize this as a large circle, I hope. This represents "Fraud." And inside we'll put smaller circles: "False Pretenses," "False Representations," "Outright Lies," "Half-truths," "Deliberate Concealment of Important Information," "Misleading Representations," "Statements Made with Reckless Indifference to Their Truth."

There are two things you'll notice about this diagram. The first is that the circles overlap. Not because I can't draw—although I can't—but because the types of fraud do, in fact, overlap. Almost any half-truth involves deliberate concealment, for example.

But you don't have to categorize the statements because, as you see from this important diagram, "fraud" defines a set of conduct that is larger than its individual parts. Also, fraud is a *course* of conduct—a constellation of false statements and deceptive acts that span months, even years. That's why you have to look at the evidence as a whole.

Nevertheless, it's still useful to use our matryoshka approach and look at how courts define and describe the different techniques of fraud. So here goes:

First, *False Pretenses*. One traditional instruction on fraud says that a scheme to defraud "need not misrepresent any fact." All that's required is that the scheme be "reasonably calculated to deceive persons of ordinary prudence and comprehension." You can defraud people without making any direct assertions at all.

How would someone do that? By arranging a situation to give a false impression. Example: My son's 1994 Honda Civic has a big dent on the side. Occasionally, someone will knock on the door and ask if we want it fixed. We always say, "No." But assume we say, "Sure, how much?" The guy says, "$500.00—half now and half later." So we give him $250 and he takes off, never to return.

Now that's fraud, but he hasn't *asserted* anything. He gave the impression that he would fix the dent—you could say he made implied assertions—but he never actually said it.

More often, false pretenses are like the background music, the ambiance. People who sell bogus investments, for example, will rent a fancy office, a Jaguar, buy their victims tennis bracelets, and take them to posh restaurants. Essentially, they portray themselves as wealthy because that lends credibility to their extravagant promises about the vast potential return on the investments they're selling. Unfortunately, however, these con artists are usually spending the unsuspecting targets' own money to dazzle them. After luring their marks in with false promises, the fraudster will seal the deal by creating a false sense of urgency: "Limited-time offer! Only three more hours!"

You're going to hear about the Bush administration's concerted efforts to set up such a false pretense regarding the alleged threat from Iraq. They created a heightened atmosphere of fear and then—like so many other criminal fraud defendants—sealed the deal by claiming it was a limited-time offer: *time is not on our side.*

Next we have *False Representations*—But let's take a break first. Fifteen minutes?

• • •

3:15 P.M.

ASSISTANT U.S. ATTORNEY: All right, everybody ready?

GRAND JURORS: [nod heads]

ASSISTANT U.S. ATTORNEY: *False Representations.* These would include outright lies, of course, as well as half-truths, such as this one from the Enron case: In the fall of 2001, when Enron was failing, Ken Lay tried to convince his employees to buy stock by telling them that he had bought $4 million in stock that very month. What he didn't mention was that he had also *sold $24 million.* The investors and employees would probably have appreciated knowing the other half of that story.

Third, *Misleading Representations.* A very effective form of fraud: Making statements that are literally true, or technically true, but wording them in a way, or stating them in a context, that is misleading and therefore false and fraudulent.

Here's a good example. In early September 2001, Lay was told that Enron was vulnerable to a corporate takeover, but when an employee asked him about it later that month, he said he had "no information" that a corporate takeover was a possibility. Under questioning by prosecutor John Hueston, Lay said, in effect, that this response had been technically true, because Lay had no information about a *specific* company planning a takeover.

I'll read you an excerpt of the cross to give you the idea. After Lay admitted that he had discussed Enron's vulnerability to a takeover in meetings with a stock analyst, Hueston asked:

> Q. And you felt at that time, then, based on what they said, that Enron was vulnerable to takeover; correct?
>
> A. I thought what they were telling me at that meeting—certainly, it was worth sharing that with my board of directors, and letting my board of directors make their own judgment as to whether we were vulnerable to a takeover or not and what to do about it.
>
> Q. Okay. [At the September 26th employees' meeting], Stephen Wolff asked: "Mr. Lay, if you can comment on this, is there any truth to the possibility of Enron being acquired by another company?"
>
> And there's a response here. You chose to reply, did you not, sir?
>
> A. I did.
>
> Q. *And you said, "I certainly have no information or expectation that any other company might be considering acquiring Enron." Those were your words; correct?"*

A. *And, again, I'm talking about any specific companies' interest in acquiring or merging with Enron.*

ASSISTANT U.S. ATTORNEY: So you see, Lay was trying to say his statement was literally true—

GRAND JUROR: Yo!

ASSISTANT U.S. ATTORNEY: Yo?

GRAND JUROR: Wasn't that, like, an outright lie? He talked about it with the Goldman Sachs guy, with the board of directors . . . If you ask me, that's, like, a lie.

ASSISTANT U.S. ATTORNEY: Well, either way, it's misleading and therefore fraudulent.

Another classic way to deceive is by juxtaposing two statements in a way that suggests some logical or causal relationship, even though there is none. Some of you may remember the old Listerine label that claimed: "Kills Germs by Millions on Contact. For General Oral Hygiene, Bad Breath, Colds, and Resultant Sore Throats."

Most people who read that thought, *Great, Listerine will help prevent or cure colds and sore throats.* A reasonable conclusion, but not true. So enter the FTC, which found the ad deceptive: "By placing these two statements in close proximity, [the manufacturer] has conveyed the message that since Listerine can kill millions of germs, it can cure, prevent and ameliorate colds and sore throats." That was the end of that ad.

GRAND JUROR: Is that like talking about 9/11 and Saddam Hussein in the same breath all the time?

ASSISTANT U.S. ATTORNEY: Exactly.

OK, *False Promises.* False predictions or promises are considered fraudulent when the defendant either: (1) did not himself believe they were true; (2) had no reasonable factual basis for making them; or (3) knowingly concealed adverse, material information when he made them.

As applied to this case, then, even if White House officials subjectively believed their own statements about Iraq, did they have a reasonable basis for making them? Or, even if they subjectively thought their claims were true, did they conceal adverse information that the public was entitled to know at the time they made them? No one is entitled to persuade others through baseless assertions or half-truths, simply because he personally, for whatever reason, believes they're true.

What is *Deliberate Concealment of Material Information?* Fraud also includes concealing information that the target of the representation wouldn't think, or even know enough, to ask about. If someone sells you a used plasma-screen TV, for instance, you assume he owns it. But if he fails to mention having stolen the TV—and what thieves would—then he has deliberately concealed the material fact that he's not authorized to sell the TV.

You might find this concept applicable to this case as well. The evidence will show, I believe, that after the invasion of Iraq, when no WMD were found, the President attempted to blame his misrepresentations about prewar intelligence on the Central Intelligence Agency, the CIA. White House officials claimed they had merely been relaying intelligence from the CIA and the CIA's reports had been wrong. *Darn it.*

Let's assume for the heck of it that the President and his advisers were merely talking heads relaying information that they had neither evaluated nor confirmed. The next issue, then, is whether their failure to inquire about the basis for their statements was a material fact that they should have disclosed to Congress and the American public. If, for example, Bush was claiming that he "knew" Iraq was seeking nuclear weapons based solely on a one-page summary given to him by the CIA, was he obligated to disclose the limited nature of his information?

The law of fraud takes into account the public's right to make certain assumptions about statements made by people who hold themselves out as authorities, such as experts, corporate officers, and high public officials. The public assumes, and is legally entitled to assume, that persons in authority will not assert facts without first thoroughly vetting them. If people make assertions about important matters without performing that due diligence, knowing and intending that the public will rely upon them, they have committed fraud.

Which leads to our final category: *Statements Made with Reckless Indifference to Their Truth*. In criminal law, false representations include ones made with "reckless indifference as to their truth or falsity."

GRAND JUROR: Is "falsity" the opposite of "truthiness?"

ASSISTANT U.S. ATTORNEY: I don't believe the Supreme Court has ruled on that . . .

But as to reckless disregard, this is just the other side of the coin of deliberate concealment of material facts. Making a statement without even trying to find out *what* the basis is also constitutes fraud. A reasonable basis, by the way, does not mean that someone, anyone, anywhere, has said a certain thing. All relevant facts, including adverse information, must be taken into account.

So this is the legal question you will be deciding:

> Is there probable cause to believe that the defendants used deceit, craft, trickery, dishonest means—including lies, false pretenses, misrepresentations, deliberate omissions, half-truths, false promises, and statements made with reckless indifference to their truth—to obstruct, impede, or interfere with Congress' lawful government function of overseeing foreign affairs, relating to the invasion of Iraq?

We'll see you all tomorrow at 9:00 A.M. Our witness tomorrow will be an FBI agent. She's from Boston, but we should be able to get by without a translator.

Have a good evening.

END OF DAY ONE

UNITED STATES v. GEORGE W. BUSH et al. GRAND JURY PRESENTATION

Testimony of FBI Special Agent Linda Campbell

ASSISTANT U.S. ATTORNEY: Good morning everyone. We're back here in the case of *United States* v. *George W. Bush et al.* Let's start by looking at Exhibit 1 in your packets.

GRAND JUROR: We were hoping you'd draw another Venn Diagram.

ASSISTANT U.S. ATTORNEY: I'm never going to live that down, am I? Has everyone got the exhibit? It's a chart that lists the main points we're going to cover in the grand jury.

Ex. 1
Evolution of the Fraud

- Bush, Cheney, et al. were predisposed to invade Iraq even before they were elected.
- They secretly began to plan the invasion immediately after September 11. Bush requested an Iraq war plan in November 2001 and began escalating military activity.
- They enlisted biased political appointees to find evidence to justify a war beginning in October 2001.
- They began, without a reasonable basis, to imply that Iraq was linked to the September 11

attacks and posed an urgent threat in the fall of 2001.

- They began a massive fraud campaign in September 2002 to overcome weak public support for an invasion and manipulate Congress into passing an authorization allowing the President to use force against Iraq.
- They invaded Iraq in March 2003, knowing that their stated grounds for war were false, fraudulent, and without reasonable basis.

Today, we'll talk about the administration's predisposition to invade Iraq.

Now, why is that relevant? Remember I told you that many fraud conspiracies begin as legitimate enterprises? They evolve into criminal activity when people begin to deceive others in response to problems or obstacles to achieving their goals. So, in any fraud case we need to know what the defendants' original objectives were.

Would somebody go get our witness? Thanks. [Whereupon the witness enters the room and is sworn]

Q. Could you please tell us your full name and what you do?

A. My name is Linda Marie Campbell and I'm a Special Agent with the FBI—have been for sixteen years.

Q. What is your current assignment?

A. I'm one of eight agents on the task force that's investigating whether the President and his senior advisers defrauded Americans about prewar intelligence. But normally my office is in Boston. Home of Tom Brady—the Patriot—and of course, Sam Adams—the beer *and* the patriot—with a small "p." I do fraud cases, mainly.

Q. Could you tell us about your background? Sort of a *Reader's Digest* version?

A. Sure. I was an Air Force brat, so we lived all over—Georgia, Germany, Hawaii—until I was about twelve, when we landed at Otis Air Force Base on Cape Cod. After Boston College, I started teaching English at Catholic Memorial. I was going to coach softball, go down the Cape in the summer, eat fried clams. But one day I just thought, *you know*, *I really can't stand talking about Hester Prynne for one more minute*, and it seemed as if it would be wicked cool to become an FBI agent. So I applied.

Q. Has it been wicked cool?

A. Yes and no. One thing about the FBI is that they always send you somewhere that's *not* where you want to be, even if no one else *does* want to be where you want to be. Does that make any sense? So I asked to go to Boston after Quantico . . .

Q. And where'd they send you?

A. Tulsa, Oklahoma. But only for two years, because I took a language aptitude test and, next thing I knew, I was at the Monterey Defense Language Institute, learning Russian. I worked in DC for a few years and finally got back to Boston last summer. Although, now I'm in DC again working on this case. I'm also on the Emergency Response and Disaster Recovery Team.

Not exactly condensed was it?

Q. No, but that's ok. You were, in fact, part of the team at the Pentagon after 9/11, weren't you?

A. Yes, I was. I will never forget it.

Q. Jurors, you recall that you may only consider evidence your hear from the witnesses? That means we occasionally present testimony about things people already know.

Like, in this case, September 11, 2001. What happened on that day?

A. On September 11, nineteen men hijacked four commercial airplanes—United Flight 175 and American Airlines 11 out of Logan, United Flight 93 out of Newark, and American Airlines 77 out of Washington/Dulles. They crashed two planes into the World Trade Towers in New York and one into the Pentagon. The fourth plane, United Flight 93, crashed in Pennsylvania after the passengers stormed the cockpit. In all, nearly 3,000 people were killed. It was a nightmare.

Q. Were you working at the time?

A. I was at firearms training, but I called my supervisor and told him I'd go wherever they needed me for disaster response. By 5:00 P.M., I'm headed to DC on the Mass Pike, with my Dunkin' Donuts iced coffee. One of the four essential food groups, by the way.

Q. Did you already know who committed the attacks?

A. Basically, yes. By late morning, really, everyone was talking about it having been al Qaeda and, of course, Osama Bin Laden. It was even on the radio. No specifics, but it was only a day or so before we heard those. The main hijacker was Mohamed Atta, who, along with 14 others, was from Saudi Arabia. Two were from Yemen and two were from Lebanon.

Q. We'll have more about this later, but—bottom line—was there ever any evidence that Saddam Hussein was involved in the September 11 hijackings?

A. No, not a bit.

Q. But your investigation has shown, has it not, that before the war, a majority of Americans believed that Saddam Hussein was somehow involved?

A. Yes.

Q. Danny Crain—Special Agent Crain—will be testifying about that in more detail, but in the meantime, have you determined how people came to believe that?

A. Unfortunately, yes. President Bush—and Cheney and Rice and Rumsfeld and Powell—deliberately gave people that impression, or allowed them to have it. That's Danny's area of testimony, I know, but let me say this: In fraud cases, we don't have to prove that people were actually deceived, but the case is stronger when you can prove they were. And here we know that many people came to believe many things about Iraq that were just false—including that there was some 9/11 connection.

Q. Well, let's turn to—

A. May I just add something?

Q. Of course.

A. Sometimes, the best way to understand the impact of fraud is not so much the number of victims, but the stories of the victims. Like in the movie *Why We Fight*, Wilton Sekzer. He was a retired cop whose son died in the World Trade Center. He strongly supported the war against Iraq, but only because he thought it was related to 9/11.

So, in 2004, when the President said not only that he had no evidence linking Saddam to the 9/11 attacks, but also "I don't know where people got the idea that I connected Iraq to 9/11," Mr. Sekzer was devastated. I'll read what he said:

> What did he [Bush] just say? I mean, I almost jumped out of the chair. *I don't know where people got the idea that I connected Iraq to 9/11*. What is he, nuts or what? What the hell did we go in there for? We're getting back for 9/11. Well, if he didn't have anything to do with 9/11, why did we go in there? I was mad. I was mad. My first thought is: you know, you're a liar.

Q. And he felt betrayed?

A. Absolutely.

Q. Was he the only one?

A. No. As of July 2003, approximately 71 percent of the people in the United States believed that the President had deliberately implied that there was a link between 9/11 and Saddam Hussein.

•••

11:00 A.M.

ASSISTANT U.S. ATTORNEY: How's the temperature? I got GSA to turn off the air conditioning.

GRAND JUROR: No kidding. Now it's way too hot.

SECOND GRAND JUROR: Are we allowed to vote someone off the Grand Jury?

Q. It's tempting.

Agent Campbell, what evidence shows that Bush et al. were predisposed to invade Iraq before January 2001?

A. Well, we have to start back in 1992, after the first Gulf War.

Q. Ok. We're not going anywhere.

A. As some jurors may know, the ground-assault phase of the first Gulf War had ended after a hundred hours, because George H. W. Bush decided not to send troops on into Baghdad. Afterward, there was a bloodbath as Saddam Hussein put down a Shiite rebellion in southern Iraq.

At the time, at least publicly, Cheney, who was Secretary of Defense, supported Bush Sr.'s decision. He said if we'd gone into Baghdad, we'd still have forces there and we would be running the country. Cheney didn't think Saddam Hussein was worth "that damned many" casualties, meaning more than the 146 American soldiers who had already died.

Q. Does it appear that Cheney later changed his mind?

A. Yes. But Libby and Wolfowitz disagreed from the beginning.

Q. Who are Libby and Wolfowitz?

A. Libby is I. Lewis Libby, Cheney's aide in 1992. In 2001 he became a top adviser, mainly on foreign-policy issues, for Cheney and also for Bush. Until he got indicted. Paul Wolfowitz was also Cheney's aide in 1992 and in 2001 became Rumsfeld's Deputy Secretary of Defense.

Libby, Wolfowitz, and Cheney had a foreign-policy philosophy that's been described as neoconservative. They first wrote about it, as far as we know, in a 1992 paper called "Defense Planning Guidance." It was never published, but the draft was leaked to the press, so we know its main points. They wanted the United States to "assert world dominance" and to "to punish" or "threaten to punish" possible future aggressors to protect U.S. access to Persian Gulf oil or stop the proliferation of WMD—weapons of mass destruction. They also recommended that the United States ignore the UN Security Council and act alone if it chose to do so.

Q. How were those ideas received at the time?

A. About as well as Stephen Colbert at the White House Correspondents' dinner.

Q. Not a warm reception, I take it. So what happened to "Defense Policy Guidance"?

A. Cheney, Wolfowitz, and Libby published a watered-down version of it in 1993 called "Defense Strategy for the 1990s."

Q. Did other future Bush-Cheney administration members publicly state their positions about the Middle East and/or Iraq in the 1990s?

A. Yes, they did. In 1996 Richard Perle, Douglas Feith, and David Wurmser wrote a paper for the Israeli government, called "A Clean Break: A New Strategy for Securing the

Realm," that advocated invading Iraq to remove Saddam Hussein.

Q. And how did those three figure in the Bush-Cheney administration?

A. From 2001 to 2003, Perle was Chairman of Bush's Defense Policy Board. Feith was Bush's Undersecretary of Defense for Policy and Wurmser was brought in after 9/11 as part of the Counter Terrorism Evaluation Group that reviewed raw intelligence looking for evidence of links between Iraq and al Qaeda or Osama Bin Laden.

Q. In 1997, there was—

A. Also, oh, sorry—

Q. No, go ahead. But if we both talk at the same time, the court reporter might quit.

A. What I was going to say was that David Wurmser also publicly advocated a United States invasion of Iraq. Twice, actually. Once in a 1997 *Wall Street Journal* editorial and then in a November 2000 *Washington Times* op-ed, where he argued that the United States and Israel should "strike fatally, not merely disarm, the centers of radicalism in the region—the regimes of Damascus, Baghdad, Tripoli, Tehran, and Gaza."

GRAND JUROR: Someone who had publicly advocated using military force to remove Saddam Hussein *and* attacking Syria, Libya, Iran, and Gaza was assigned to look for evidence to justify invading Iraq?

A. Yes. He is now Vice President Cheney's adviser on the Middle East.

Q. All right. In 1997, a group called Project for a New American Century, or PNAC, was formed. What was that?

A. According to its website, PNAC is a think tank dedicated to "American global leadership." Its stated principles were: (1) promoting a bold foreign policy; (2) significantly increasing defense spending; and (3) meeting threats "before they become dire."

Cheney, Rumsfeld, Libby, and Wolfowitz were founding members, as was Jeb Bush, President Bush's brother.

Q. Did the founding statement mention Iraq?

A. No, but a letter the members of PNAC wrote to Clinton in 1998 did.

Q. Before we get to that, were there other public statements advocating forcible removal of Saddam Hussein made by future Bush-Cheney people in 1997?

A. Yes, in a December 1997 issue of the *Weekly Standard* magazine called "Saddam Must Go: A How-to Guide," Wolfowitz and the current U.S. ambassador to Iraq, Zalmay Khalilzad, called for "sustained attacks" on Hussein's military and security forces to get rid of him.

Q. Early in 1998, the Project for a New American Century wrote the letter you just mentioned, right?

A. Right. Yes, most of it is excerpted in Exhibit 2:

Ex. 2
Excerpts from January 26, 1998 Letter from PNAC to President William J. Clinton

We are writing you because we are convinced that current American policy toward Iraq is not succeeding and that we may soon face a threat in the Middle East more serious than any we have known since the end of the Cold War. . . . We urge you to . . . enunciate a new strategy . . . [that] should aim, above all, at the removal of Saddam Hussein's regime from power. . . .

The policy of "containment" of Saddam Hussein has been steadily eroding over the past several months. . . .

It hardly needs to be added that if Saddam does acquire the capability to deliver weapons of mass destruction, as he is almost certain to do if we continue along the present course, the safety of American troops in the region, of our friends and allies like Israel and the moderate Arab states, and a significant portion of the world's supply of oil will all be put at hazard. As you have rightly declared, Mr. President, the security of the world in the first part of the 21st century will be determined largely by how we handle this threat.

Given the magnitude of the threat, the current policy, which depends for its success upon the steadfastness of our coalition partners and upon the cooperation of Saddam Hussein, is dangerously inadequate. The only acceptable strategy is

> one that eliminates the possibility that Iraq will be able to use or threaten to use weapons of mass destruction. In the near term, this means a willingness to undertake military action as diplomacy is clearly failing. In the long term, it means removing Saddam Hussein and his regime from power.
>
> In any case, American policy cannot continue to be crippled by a misguided insistence on unanimity in the UN Security Council.

Q. Any familiar names in the signature block?

A. Twelve of the eighteen signers became Bush-Cheney advisers or appointees: Rumsfeld, Wolfowitz, John Bolton, Khalilzad, Perle, as well as Elliot Abrams, Richard Armitage, Paula Dobriansky, Peter Rodman, R. James Woolsey, and Robert Zoellick.

Q. Well, it's 12:30 and I'm "stahvin," as Agent Campbell would say. So let's go eat.

•••

1:30 P.M.

ASSISTANT U.S. ATTORNEY: Did everyone make it back? Good.

GRAND JUROR: Agent Campbell, doesn't this 1998 letter contain the same arguments that the Bush administration made in 2002?

A. Yes it does: (1) containment wasn't working; (2) inspections wouldn't work; (3) Saddam would definitely have

WMD if we didn't act immediately; and (4) we didn't need to work with the UN.

GRAND JUROR: What does "containment" mean?

A. In the context of Iraq, it referred mainly to the use of UN sanctions and restrictions to prevent Saddam Hussein from acquiring WMD and from threatening his neighbors.

Q. We're going to switch gears and turn to the 2000 election campaign. Before that, any questions?

GRAND JUROR: Was Bush in PNAC?

A. No. But in 1999, he hired Condoleezza Rice and her future Deputy National Security Adviser, Stephen Hadley, along with five PNAC people—Perle, Wolfowitz, Armitage, Zoellick, and Dov Zakheim—to be campaign foreign policy advisers. Four of those five had previously advocated forcibly removing Saddam Hussein.

Q. During the 2000 campaign, did Bush and Cheney talk about U.S. global preeminence and taking preventive military action against possible threats from WMD or to our oil interests in the Middle East?

A. No. Well, yes and no.

Q. Oh, okay. Everybody got that, then?

A. Well, behind the scenes, with the neoconservative crowd, Bush and Cheney conveyed a very strong message. In fact, in September 2000 Libby, Wolfowitz, and ten other future Bush-Cheney appointees signed a policy statement, called "Rebuilding America's Defenses," that was posted on the PNAC website. The paper, which described itself as a "blueprint for maintaining global U.S. preeminence" that grew out of Cheney's 1992 "Defense Policy Guidance" paper, advocated substantially increased defense spending. Regarding the Middle East, it said the "need for a substantial American force presence in the Gulf transcends the issue of the regime of Saddam Hussein."

In plain English: We should have permanent military bases in the Middle East.

Q. Did the statement indicate whether PNAC thought the public would agree with this strategy?

A. Yes. PNAC acknowledged that its goals would likely take a long time to achieve, "absent some catastrophic and catalyzing event—like a new Pearl Harbor."

Q. Anyone could look at this website, couldn't they?

A. Yes. But it was not well known outside of DC and certain conservative circles, and publicly, especially in the general election, Bush and Cheney said nothing whatsoever about a "bold" foreign policy or any other PNAC principles.

Q. Can you give us some examples?

A. Sure. On August 27, 2000, on *Meet the Press*, Cheney said that the U.S. should not act as "an imperialist power, willy-nilly moving into capitals in that part of the world, taking down governments." He was talking about the Middle East.

Also, in the presidential debate against Al Gore at UMass on October 3, Bush said he would "take the use of force very seriously" and "be guarded" in his approach. He also said he disagreed with Vice President Gore about the use of troops: "He [Gore] believes in nation building. I would be very careful about using our troops as nation-builders."

Then, in the October 11 debate, Bush was asked how the

world should view us and he said they would welcome us "if we're a humble nation, but strong." He also said we needed to "project strength in a way that promotes freedom."

Q. What did Bush say about the need for building coalitions?

A. One of Bush's main themes was that he was a leader and that leaders build coalitions. On December 2, 1999, for example, he said he would "keep the peace" by "strengthening alliances, which says [*sic*] America cannot go alone, we must be peacemakers not peacekeepers." In the October 11 debate, he said, "It's important to have credibility and credibility is formed by being strong with your friends and resoluting [*sic*] your determination." It was especially important to have strong ties in the Middle East, he said, because of the oil there.

Q. Did Bush or Cheney talk about forcibly removing Saddam Hussein during the 2000 campaign?

A. Cheney never did, but early on, Bush seemed to say just that, perhaps inadvertently. In the December 2, 1999, New Hampshire Republican primary debate, the Fox News reporter Brit Hume asked him what he would do differently from Clinton regarding Saddam Hussein. And Bush said:

> I wouldn't ease the [U.N.] sanctions, and I wouldn't try to negotiate with him. I'd make darn sure that he lived up to the agreements that he signed back in the early '90s. I'd be helping the opposition groups. And if I found in any way, shape or form that he was developing weapons of mass destruction, I'd take 'em out. I'm surprised he's still there. I think a lot of other people are as well.

Now, it's odd. The transcript says "'em"—and I have no idea who's responsible for that. But, at the time, Hume clearly thought Bush was referring to "him," as in Saddam Hussein. And he—Hume, I mean—said, "Take *him* out?" And Bush responded, "To out [*sic*] the weapons of mass destruction." Which did not follow from saying "I'm surprised he's still there."

Q. Did Bush ever say "take 'em out" relating to Iraq or Saddam Hussein again during the campaign?

A. No. Although, in February 2000, he said, "There won't be any weapons of mass destruction left in Iraq if I'm the Commander-in-Chief." Usually, though, when Bush talked about Iraq, he'd say something like achieving world peace would require "firmness with regimes like North Korea and Iraq."

Actually, when you look carefully at what he said, he conveyed almost no information whatsoever.

Q. Have you come across a notable instance where Bush used the term "Commander-in-Chief"?

A. Yes. In May 1999, during an interview with a family friend and reporter named Mickey Herskovitz for a campaign book that someone else ended up writing, Bush said, "One of the keys to being seen as a great leader is to be seen as a Commander-in-Chief." He also said:

> My father had all this political capital built up when he drove the Iraqis out of Kuwait and he wasted it. If I have a chance to invade—if I had that much capital, I'm not going to waste it. I'm

> going to get everything passed that I want to get passed and I'm going to have a successful presidency.

GRAND JUROR: In other words, Bush was saying that the way to be seen as a great leader was to start a war?

A. It appears so.

Q. Let's take our afternoon break.

•••

3:15 P.M.

ASSISTANT U.S. ATTORNEY: Special Agent Campbell, you mentioned that numerous advocates of the Project for a New American Century principles relating to U.S. global dominance and preventive attacks ended up in the Bush-Cheney administration in 2001.

How many of the people brought in by Bush, Cheney, and Rumsfeld were public proponents of the PNAC principles?

A. Public proponents of the PNAC principles?

Q. Precisely.

A. At least twenty-eight, including advisers and consultants, as well as officials, appointees, and staff. They're all listed in Exhibit 3.

Q. Does everyone have Exhibit 3?

Ex. 3
Public Proponents of PNAC Principles

1. Paul Wolfowitz: Deputy Secretary of Defense;

2. I. Lewis Libby: Assistant to the President/ Vice President's Chief of Staff;
3. Eliot Abrams: Assistant to the President/ Deputy National Security Adviser for Global Security;
4. Stephen Cambone: Former Deputy Undersecretary of Defense for Policy/current Undersecretary of Defense for Intelligence [newly created position];
5. Richard Armitage: Deputy Secretary of State;
6. Christopher Williams: Special Assistant to the Secretary of Defense;
7. John Bolton: UN Ambassador/Former Undersecretary of Defense for Arms Control and International Security;
8. Peter Rodman: Assistant Director of Defense for National Security Affairs;
9. Paula Dobriansky: Undersecretary of Defense for Democracy and Global Affairs;
10. Douglas Feith: Former Undersecretary of Defense for Policy;
11. David Wurmser: Middle East Adviser to the VP/Former Special Adviser to the Undersecretary of State for Arms Control and International Security;
12. Abram Shulsky: Director of Defense Department's Office of Special Plans;
13. Zalmay Khalilzad: Ambassador to Iraq/Former Special Assistant to the President for Persian Gulf Affairs;

14. Barry Watts: Office of the Secretary of Defense/Director of Program Analysis & Evaluation;
15. Dov Zakheim: Undersecretary and Chief Financial for Defense Department;
16. Mark Lagon: Deputy Assistant Secretary of State;
17. Robert B. Zoellick: Former U.S. Trade Representative/Former Deputy National Security Adviser;
18. David Epstein: Staff, Secretary of Defense;
19. Richard Perle: Former Chairman, Defense Policy Board;
20. Eliot Cohen: Defense Policy Board;
21. Devon Gaffney-Cross: Defense Policy Board;
22. Henry S. Rowen: Defense Policy Board;
23. R. James Woolsey: Defense Policy Board;
24. Richard V. Allen: Defense Policy Board;
25. Daniel Goure: Consultant to Secretary of Defense;
26. Gary Shmitt: Consultant to Secretary of Defense;
27. Randy Scheuneman: Consultant to Secretary of Defense;
28. William Schneider, Jr.: Chairman, Defense Science Board

Q. Out of those, how many had specifically and publicly called for the use of United States military force to depose Saddam Hussein?

A. Seventeen. The underlined names are people who had already called for the forcible removal of Saddam Hussein.

Q. Those would include the Deputy Secretaries of Defense and State, as well as seven additional high-level appointees in the State and Defense Departments, correct?

A. Yes. Also, of course, Defense Secretary Rumsfeld. Including Rumsfeld, eighteen of the Bush-Cheney administration appointees had publicly called for the removal of Saddam Hussein before 2001, including Rumsfeld.

GRAND JUROR: The evidence about Project for a New American Century, and Bush talking about being a Commander-in-Chief?

Q. Yes?

GRAND JUROR: Are you saying that Bush and Cheney were definitely planning to invade Iraq from the beginning?

Q. No, and that is not something you have to decide in this case. The predisposition evidence shows the genesis and some of the motivation for the fraud, but it's not intended to be proof of the fraud itself. You could decide they were *not* predisposed to invade Iraq and still find probable cause to believe that they conspired to defraud the United States beginning on or before September 2002.

So, let's call it a day. Thank you for your testimony, Agent Campbell. Have a good evening, everyone.

END OF DAY TWO

UNITED STATES v. GEORGE W. BUSH et al.
GRAND JURY PRESENTATION

Testimony of FBI Special Agent
Joseph Estrada

9:00 A.M.

ASSISTANT U.S. ATTORNEY DE LA VEGA: Here we are again. Could someone go get our witness? [Whereupon the witness enters the room and was sworn]

Q. Good morning.

A. Good morning!!!

Q. Sounds like James Earl Jones, doesn't he? Could you please tell us your full name?

A. Joseph Aurelio Munoz Estrada.

Q. And we dragged you here from Sacramento to help out, didn't we?

A. Yeah. Actually Petaluma—where they filmed *American Graffiti*. So you've probably seen Petaluma, even if you've never heard of it.

Q. Could you tell us about your background—in twenty-five words or less?

A. Studied psychology and criminal justice at Sonoma State. Cop for six years. Never ate a single doughnut. Attended law school at night. Became an FBI agent. Have done all kinds of cases.

Q. Pretty good. Thirty-two words.

Moving on, Special Agent Campbell testified yesterday about the dichotomy between Bush-Cheney's public campaign statements and their behind-the-scenes policies, especially in light of the views of so many of their senior appointees. Is it illegal for a candidate to defraud people about his policies during the campaign?

A. No. But once he's elected, he's no longer—for legal purposes—"just" a politician. He's a United States government official.

Q. On what day did Bush stop being "just" a politician?

A. January 20, 2001. The day he took the Presidential Oath of Office.

Q. What was the oath that Bush swore to uphold?

A. The one from the United States Constitution:

> I do solemnly swear (or affirm) that I will faithfully execute the office of President of the United States, and will to the best of my ability, preserve, protect, and defend the Constitution of the United States.

Q. Is there another provision that imposes legal obligations upon the president?

A. Yes, the Constitution requires the president to "take care that the laws be faithfully executed."

Q. Just certain ones, or all of them?

A. All of them.

Q. Is there also another source of legal obligations that applies to the president?

A. Yes. Bush, Cheney, Rice, Rumsfeld, and Powell are all subject to Executive Orders 12674 and 12731, which provide that Executive Branch employees hold their positions as a public trust and Americans have a right to expect that they will fulfill that trust according to certain ethical standards and principles. Including, obviously, abiding by the Constitution and U.S. laws.

Q. Were the other defendants also sworn in on January 20, 2001?

A. Yes, or thereabouts. Dick Cheney was sworn in as Vice President. Condoleezza Rice was sworn in as National Security Adviser; Donald Rumsfeld as Secretary of Defense; and Colin Powell as Secretary of State. And they took the same oath as the President: To faithfully execute their offices and to preserve, protect, and defend the laws and Constitution of the United States.

Q. So as of January 20, 2001, the President and his advisers assumed the same obligations of truthfulness, forthrightness, and honesty toward the public with regard to matters of governance that the Enron officials had with regard to corporate matters?

A. Exactly.

Q. Let's turn now to January 2001. Agent Estrada, could you, briefly, describe the Bush administration's approach to Iraq at that point?

A. Conflicted.

Q. Not *that* briefly.

A. Okay. Iraq was an extremely high priority, far more so

than under Clinton. Early on, Bush and Cheney met with outgoing President Bill Clinton and, separately, with Clinton's outgoing Secretary of Defense William Cohen. In each meeting, they stressed that their top foreign policy priority was Iraq.

Then, shortly before his inauguration, Bush started upping the ante publicly. He called Saddam a "wild card" who might destabilize world oil supplies. And when asked whether he'd use military force against Saddam, he said, "If he [Hussein] crosses the line. . . . If we catch him developing weapons of mass destruction, the answer's yes."

Q. Was there evidence that Saddam Hussein was developing WMD in January 2001?

A. No. Intelligence assessments in effect at that time said Saddam might have some biological and chemical weapons, but no nuclear weapons, or even nuclear-weapons capability, although intelligence agencies believed Saddam had the desire to get them. Both Colin Powell and Donald Rumsfeld stated publicly in 2001 that Saddam Hussein's regime had no nuclear program. Powell, Rice, and Rumsfeld also said publicly that the previous administration's policy of containment had worked. In fact, Powell said, Saddam's ground forces were so degraded as a result of the UN sanctions that had been in effect since 1991 that he couldn't attack his neighbors. Powell did say, however, that Saddam might be trying to develop chemical and biological weapons to compensate for his weak conventional force.

Saddam was, Powell said, a threat to his neighbors, but not to the United States. So on February 4, 2001, when Sam Donaldson, of ABC's *This Week*, asked Powell about

Bush's "take 'em out" comment from December 2, 1999, all Powell said was that we "reserve the right to use whatever means necessary" if we had specific targets or if "something occurred to us."

Q. What had Donaldson's question been?

A. Whether Powell was saying he did not "have enough evidence to believe that you should follow through on President Bush's words to take out those weapons."

Q. Is it fair to say that Bush, Rice, and Rumsfeld did not have the same public position as Powell?

A. Yes. They admitted that Iraq was contained, but nevertheless began referring to Saddam as a threat, not just to his neighbors, but to the entire world, including, presumably, the United States.

Q. What happened on February 11, three weeks after Bush's inauguration?

A. Bush authorized strikes outside the Iraq no-fly zones for the first time since 1998. Twenty-four American and British planes struck five Iraqi military targets five to twenty miles from Baghdad, using long-range precision-guided weapons.

GRAND JUROR: Why did Bush do that?

A. Bush said he wanted to send Saddam Hussein a "clear message" that his administration would be "engaged in that part of the world." He said that mission had been accomplished: "We got his attention."

Bush said he also wanted to degrade Saddam's capacity to harm any pilots we had flying in the no-fly zone.

Q. Was it a one-time thing?

A. No. Bombings in and outside the no-fly zones continued and eventually increased in 2002.

Q. What were the no-fly zones?

A. They were areas of Iraq designated by the United States, Great Britain, and France after the Gulf War, to protect Kurds in the north and Shiites in the south from attacks by Saddam Hussein.

Q. Were there other changes with regard to Iraq in the first nine months of 2001?

A. Behind the scenes, Bush's people began to replace career foreign-intelligence personnel assigned to Iraq issues with their own personal appointees. Or, sometimes, they just left the career people out of the loop. But that's what Danny Crain's going to testify about tomorrow.

Also, publicly, Bush got increasingly aggressive about foreign policy. Here are excerpts from a speech he gave on May 1, 2001:

> Unlike the Cold War, today's most urgent threat stems . . . from a small number of missiles in the hands of these states ["the least responsible states"] for whom terror and blackmail are a way of life. They seek weapons of mass destruction to intimidate their neighbors, and to keep the United States and other responsible nations from helping allies and friends in strategic parts of the world.
>
> When Saddam Hussein invaded Kuwait in 1990, the world joined forces to turn him back.

> But the international community would have faced a very different situation had Hussein been able to blackmail with nuclear weapons. Like Saddam Hussein, some of today's tyrants are gripped by an implacable hatred of the United States of America. They hate our friends, they hate our values, they hate democracy and freedom and individual liberty. Many care little for the lives of their own people. In such a world, Cold War deterrence is no longer enough.

Q. This was May of 2001?

A. Yes.

Q. So even *before* 9/11, Bush was saying that our most urgent threat comes from missiles in the hands of "the least responsible states" for whom blackmail and terror are a way of life?

A. Yes.

Q. And implying that Saddam had nuclear weapons?

A. Yes. If you look at the second paragraph, sentences two and three, you can see that they constitute a classic misrepresentation—nothing untrue, but misleading because of the phrasing and juxtaposition of ideas.

GRAND JUROR: Like the Listerine ad.

A. First Bush talks about *what if*, in essence, Saddam *had* been "able to blackmail with nuclear weapons."

Now this is a presidential speech. So it goes through five, ten, twenty drafts, and Bush has made a big point of emphasizing that he has "hands-on" involvement in making sure his speeches are written the way he wants.

Q. Could you give us some examples?

A. Sure. On May 2, 2003, Bush's Director of Global Communications Tucker Eskew was asked in an online chat, "How involved is President Bush at editing or changing the copy?" And this was Eskew's answer:

> [I]n general, especially for major addresses, it starts with Presidential direction to the speechwriters, led by Mike Gerson. They get ideas and input and re-writes from their colleagues (especially Dan Bartlett and Karen Hughes). Then, the President again sets the direction, adds and makes changes. An accurate description of his hands-on approach can be found in Woodward's *Bush at War*.

Q. And in the book, *Bush at War*, the well-known *Washington Post* reporter Bob Woodward describes how Bush provides the basic ideas, discusses drafts with aides and speechwriters, and finally does line editing, correct?

A. Yes.

Q. So getting back to Bush's May 1, 2001, speech . . .

A. Right. Now we all know that statements are in presidential speeches for a *reason*. Bush always makes local references and jokes about how he "married up," to emphasize that he is congenial, funny, and married. That's fine, of course, but the point is, the stuff is there *intentionally*.

So you know that Bush is not just randomly wondering, "Hey, what if Saddam had nuclear weapons?" like some twelve year-old at a sleepover whispering, "*What if Dr. Octopus is hiding out in the McKenzies' garage right now?*"

Yet you also know that, horrible as he is, Saddam Hussein does *not* have nuclear weapons or the ability to make them. Bush has to have known that because his aides have said so publicly. You also know that Bush is aware that Hussein's regime is considerably weakened by sanctions and that he has been effectively contained. Bush's advisers have stated that publicly as well—many times.

So this is where you use common sense and draw the reasonable inferences that the law allows and you ask yourself: Why would President Bush deliberately bring up some terrifying thing that he *knows* has no basis in fact? That he *knows* is not true?

There is only one reasonable inference: He wanted to people to think it *was* true.

GRAND JUROR: It's like this ad I keep getting in the mail: "*What if termite swarms started heading to DC from Ft. Lauderdale in April of 2007. Are you prepared?*"

A. It *is* actually like that. Neither statement is an outright lie, but both are designed to deceive. And, because Bush is the President, what he says publicly about terrifying global threats overrides what his aides say about the facts. It's like what his aides have said is the fine print and what the President says is in bold.

In this speech, in case people are not sufficiently anxious, Bush proceeds to talk about tyrants who are "gripped by an implacable hatred" of the United States, but he only mentions one: Saddam Hussein. Implacable. Can't be placated. In other words, we are *never* going to be safe from Saddam Hussein no matter what we do. You'll notice that Bush used the same terms to describe "tyrants" in May 2001 that he used after 9/11: they hate our freedom, our values, our democracy. Then, finally, Bush gets to the idea he is trying to sell.

Q. What is he trying to sell?

A. That "cold war deterrence is no longer enough." Defensive force is not enough. We need to be prepared to use *offensive* force. Not only that, we must deter anyone who even *contemplates* using weapons of terror. Since the only person he has talked about is Saddam Hussein—

GRAND JUROR: It's the PNAC principle. Preventive war.

A. Precisely. And that was May 2001.

Q. Is this a good time for lunch? See you all at 1:30.

•••

1:30 P.M.

ASSISTANT U.S. ATTORNEY: Is everyone all set? Wait a second, where's our witness? [Whereupon Special Agent Estrada enters the room]

A. Sorry, very important FBI business . . . Actually, I had to call my son. He's going white-water rafting on the American River tomorrow and I told him not to drown.

Q. Excellent advice.

Let's go on to the second point. Agent Estrada, how

soon after the September 11th attacks did Bush and his aides begin discussing an invasion of Iraq?

A. Within a couple of hours.

Q. How do you know that?

A. Well, at this point, there are numerous sources, including reports from the 9/11 Commission, the Senate Select Committee on Intelligence, Bob Woodward's *Plan of Attack*; *Cobra II*, by the *New York Times'* Michael Gordon and retired General Bernard E. Trainer; journalist Ron Suskind's *The One Percent Doctrine*; PBS's *Frontline* documentaries; the White House website; the defendants' public statements; and numerous media accounts that allow us to reconstruct the Bush administration's Iraq-related activity after 9/11.

Q. Before we get to that, was the administration up front about the Iraq war planning discussions it was having immediately after 9/11?

A. Not at all. They tried very hard to keep people from finding out about them. And they were fairly successful for several years.

Q. What was the first significant information that came out about the post-9/11 Iraq war discussions?

A. Well, in March of 2004, Richard Clarke, the former counterterrorism czar, appeared on *60 Minutes*, prior to his testimony before the 9/11 Commission and the publication of his book, *Against All Enemies*, and said that Bush had asked him to look for links between al Qaeda and Saddam Hussein's regime on September 12.

Q. How did Clarke describe the conversation?

A. He said Bush had grabbed him after a meeting and said, "I want you, as soon as you can, to go back over everything, everything. See if Saddam did this. See if he's linked in any way."

Clarke said he had told the President, essentially, *But it was al Qaeda that attacked us.* The President acknowledged that he knew that, but he wanted Clarke to "see if Saddam was involved. . . . I want to know any shred." According to Clarke, he had also informed the President that they had previously investigated possible state sponsorship of al Qaeda and found no real linkages to Iraq. Then, Clarke said, the President told him to look into Iraq and Saddam anyway.

Q. How did the Bush administration respond to Clarke's account?

A. The way they responded to any negative information: Shoot the messenger. Typically, they would call the information "old news" or suggest the critic was disgruntled or politically motivated. Often, however, they would not dispute the substance at all, although they did dispute what Clarke had said initially.

Paul O'Neill, for example, was the former Treasury Secretary whom Ron Suskind wrote about in *The Price of Loyalty*. Among other things, O'Neill had related to Suskind that Bush's first two National Security Council meetings—January 30 and February 1, 2001—had been about Iraq.

Bush's spokesperson, Scott McClellan, was asked on January 14, 2004, if O'Neill's assertions were false, and he said he did not do "book reviews," but "this" seemed to be more about "trying to justify personal views and opinions."

Q. What did that remark mean?

A. McClellan was implying that O'Neill was making these allegations because he'd been pushed out of his job as Treasury Secretary. When the reporter pressed for an answer on the substance, McClellan launched into his talking points about the President having exhausted all peaceful means before invading Iraq.

Q. So how *did* the administration respond to Clarke?

A. First they responded with a false exculpatory statement.

Q. What is that?

A. It's a false statement made by someone accused of wrongdoing to get himself off the hook. If a person lies when confronted with wrongdoing, a jury can consider that to be evidence of guilt.

In this instance, the administration first implied, falsely, that Clarke had fabricated the whole story. National Security Adviser Stephen Hadley, who was then Rice's Deputy, said on *60 Minutes*, that they had not, "quite frankly," been able to find evidence of an incident that met Clarke's description.

Q. But the conversation *had* taken place, hadn't it?

A. Yes it had. There were a number of facts that corroborated Clarke's account. For example, on September 18, Clarke submitted a memo to Rice that was specifically in response to Bush's previous request. It would be unusual to submit a response to a request that had never been made.

It turned out, also, that two people publicly corroborated Clarke's account.

Q. What was the administration's response then?

A. All of a sudden, it was, *Well, of course, Bush was asking his counterterrorism adviser for all possible information about 9/11.* They never did stop trying to discredit Clarke, though. Rice and Cheney publicly suggested that Clarke was motivated by sour grapes, because he had not been in the administration's inner circle.

GRAND JUROR: So Bush knew Clarke was telling the truth but allowed his spokespersons to attack him anyway?

A. Yes. It seemed to be a coordinated strategy.

Q. Break time. Ten minutes okay?

•••

3:10 P.M.

ASSISTANT U.S. ATTORNEY: Agent Estrada, based on the sources you listed earlier, what did transpire after the attacks?

A. Well, around noon, CIA Director George Tenet informed Rumsfeld that al Qaeda was responsible. In spite of that, at 2:40 P.M., according to notes taken by Rumsfelds's very close aide, Stephen Cambone—a PNAC member, by the way—Rumsfeld instructed General Myers to:

> find the [b]est info fast . . . judge whether good enough [to] hit S.H. at same time—not only UBL [Usama Bin Laden].

Q. Did the note say anything else?

A. It said: "Go massive. . . . Sweep it all up. Things related and not." Meaning go massive and sweep everything up to find evidence that linked Saddam Hussein with the 9/11 attacks.

Q. Anything else?

A. Yes, near the bottom it said, "Hard to get a good case."

GRAND JUROR: And you don't know whether Rumsfeld made that statement or whether it was just what Cambone thought, right?

A. That is absolutely right.

Q. Where was Bush at this point?

A. He was still flying around in Air Force One. But at 3:15 P.M., he held a videoconference with Cheney, Rice, Rumsfeld, Powell, Richard Clarke, and Tenet, who repeated the information that al Qaeda was responsible for the attacks. That night, Bush informed his "war council"—

Q. Who was on the war council?

A. The people I just mentioned, as well as General Hugh Shelton, who was Vice Chairman of the Joint Chiefs; the President's Chief of Staff, Andrew Card; FBI Director Robert Mueller; Attorney General John Ashcroft; and often Stephen Hadley and Josh Bolten, Card's Deputy. The President told them that we would go after both terrorists and those who harbored them. Rumsfeld suggested going after Iraq at that meeting too, and he wondered how much evidence we would need to justify an attack.

Q. What happened next?

A. On September 12, Bush, back in Washington, conducted two meetings with his National Security Council—the people I just mentioned—plus Clarke and Wolfowitz. And at that meeting, both Wolfowitz and Rumsfeld talked about attacking Iraq. Rumsfeld said that the United States should use 9/11 as an "opportunity."

Q. Did they say why they thought that?

A. Yes. They said that Saddam, not al Qaeda or Osama Bin Laden, should be the main target of the "war on terrorism" and that Iraq had better targets than Afghanistan. I'm not really sure what they meant by that.

Q. What did Bush say?

A. He didn't agree or disagree, but he did say that if they invaded Iraq, the goal should be to replace the Iraq government, not just to bomb the country.

Q. What were Powell's, Cheney's, and Rice's positions?

A. Powell was opposed. He didn't see a connection between Saddam and 9/11. Cheney's and Rice's position seemed to be: Whatever the President wants is what we want.

They all met over the weekend at Camp David, and Bush decided they would, for the time being, just go after Afghanistan, which was disappointing to the neoconservatives like Wolfowitz and Perle. The next day, September 17, Bush signed an order authorizing war against Afghanistan. At the same time, however, he also ordered the Defense Department to begin planning to invade Iraq.

Q. As of that day, September 17, had there been any evidence whatsoever to cause Bush or anyone else to believe that Saddam Hussein or Iraq had been involved in 9/11?

A. No.

Q. In fact, the day before, what had Cheney said about that issue on NBC's Sunday talk show, *Meet the Press*?

A. Cheney had told the host Tim Russert that the administration had no evidence linking Saddam Hussein or Iraq to 9/11.

Q. What did Bush say about the Iraq-9/11 issue around that time?

A. According to Woodward's book, *Bush at War*, Bush said to his advisers, "We have to be patient about Iraq." He said he believed Iraq was involved in 9/11 but was not going to strike them "now" because "I don't have the evidence at this point."

Q. What happened the day after Bush signed the order?

A. On September 18, Clarke's office sent National Security Adviser Condoleezza Rice the memo which summarized intelligence relating to possible Iraqi involvement in 9/11 or any Iraqi connections to al Qaeda.

Q. What did the memo say?

A. The conclusions were: One, the evidence linking Hussein to September 11 was weak; two, there was only anecdotal evidence linking Saddam to al Qaeda; three, Bin Laden resented Saddam's secularism; and four, there were no confirmed reports of Saddam and Bin Laden cooperating on WMD.

Q. Did that cause Bush to change his mind about invading Iraq?

A. No. On November 21, 2001, Bush asked Secretary of Defense Rumsfeld to provide him with a formal plan for the invasion of Iraq as soon as possible.

GRAND JUROR: Did you say November 21, *2001*? Bush asked for the Iraq war plan in *November of 2001*?

A. Yes, 2001.

Q. Okay, it's 4:30 P.M. and it has not escaped my notice that you're all checking your watches. Not to mention the "Yo" man over there has his jacket on—

GRAND JUROR: He's had it on all afternoon.

Q. How come? I thought you were too hot?

SECOND GRAND JUROR: I had a little run-in with a Whopper.

Q. Well, let's leave it here. We're a little behind, but we can catch up tomorrow if Agent Estrada will come back.

A. Happy to.

GRAND JUROR: What about Danny Crain? I thought he was going to be here tomorrow—

A. Oh, he's not that great . . .

Q. See you all in the morning.

END OF DAY THREE

UNITED STATES v. GEORGE W. BUSH et al.
GRAND JURY PRESENTATION

Testimony of FBI Special Agent
Joseph Estrada

9:00 A.M.

ASSISTANT UNITED STATES ATTORNEY: Great to see you all again. And Special Agent Estrada, thank you for coming back. [Whereupon the witness is sworn]

Q. All right then. We left off yesterday on November 21, 2001. That was the day Bush told Rumsfeld to ask CentCom Commander, General "Tommy" Franks, to give him a war plan for Iraq, correct?

A. Yes.

Q. This brings us to our third item on Exhibit 1: the President's request for an Iraq war plan and escalating military activity. First, though, what else did the President do on November 21st?

A. He went to Fort Campbell, Kentucky, and ate turkey with the "Screaming Eagles," as the 101st Airborne Division is called. Fort Campbell is, by the way, the home of the Fifth Group Special Forces.

Q. What are the Fifth Group Special Forces?

A. A group of highly trained soldiers who are fluent in Arabic, Pashtun, and Dari. In November 2001, most of them were in Afghanistan, looking for Osama Bin Laden, but in March of 2002 they were moved to Iraq.

In a speech to the troops after dinner, the President declared that Afghanistan was "just the beginning on [*sic*] the war against terror." We were going to go after all the countries that harbored terrorists.

Q. How did he end the speech?

A. "And I'm honored to be your Commander-in-Chief."

Q. As of November 21, 2001, had President Bush sought or obtained any authorization from Congress to use force against Iraq?

A. No. Bush did not seek congressional authorization to use military force until September 2002.

Q. What happened after Bush asked for the formal plan?

A. Things moved fast.

On November 27, Rumsfeld informed General Franks that the President wanted a plan to invade Iraq. On December 1, Rumsfeld put the request in a "Top Secret" order and gave Franks three days to prepare a detailed plan for an invasion of Iraq that could start within months.

Franks briefed Rumsfeld on December 4, as ordered, but Rumsfeld told him the plan needed work: Come back on December 12.

Franks came back on December 12. And Rumsfeld told him the plan needed work: Come back on December 19.

Q. Did Franks come back on the 19?

A. He sure did.

Q. What happened?

A. Rumsfeld still didn't like his plan.

GRAND JUROR: Wasn't Franks the Commander of Operations in Afghanistan at that time?

A. He sure was.

Q. Did President Bush meet with Franks about the war plan for Iraq in 2001?

A. Yes, as it was described in *Plan of Attack*—which was a book written with the full cooperation of the Bush-Cheney administration—Rumsfeld apparently told Bush that he was not pleased with Franks's successive plans, because they could not be executed quickly enough. So Bush told Rumsfeld to have Franks come to Crawford to discuss the Iraq war plan, which Franks did on December 28, 2001. He briefed the plans to Bush, Rumsfeld, Cheney, Rice, Powell, Tenet, and others, some of whom were on videoconference.

Q. What happened after the meeting?

A. Afterward, the President affirmatively misrepresented its purpose to the press. He said:

> Tommy has just come back from the Afghan theater. He gave me a full briefing on what he saw and what he heard. We just got off of a teleconference with the national security team, to discuss his trip and to discuss what's taking place in Afghanistan.

Q. Meanwhile, were we already moving military forces to the region around Iraq?

A. Starting to. On December 11, the U.S. Army moved its

Third Army Headquarters from Georgia to Kuwait. We were also increasing the number of bombing runs, widening the targets and flying more and more often outside the no-fly zones, even though we had no authority to do that. On February 3, 2002, the U.S. Marines moved their headquarters from Hawaii to Bahrain, an island in the Persian Gulf near Iraq.

Q. Was there nonmilitary preinvasion planning going on as well in early 2002?

A. Yes. Rumsfeld's Deputy Secretary Wolfowitz and Undersecretary for Policy Douglas Feith, and some of their political appointees were meeting with people from the INC.

Q. The Iraqi National Congress?

A. Correct. The INC was supplying information to the Defense Department people, and they were deeply involved with Wolfowitz and Feith making plans for postwar Iraq.

Q. Jurors, I want to mention one point. Because we're guessing that you don't want to be here indefinitely, we are not going to cover all of the defendants' fraudulent conduct. One area we won't be addressing is the defendants' reliance on the so-called intelligence that Wolfowitz, Feith, and others at the Pentagon were being fed by the informants the INC was trotting in. But briefly, Agent Estrada, could the defendants reasonably rely on that informant information?

A. They could not. For starters, Ahmed Chalabi, the INC leader, had an obvious bias in that he was dedicated to overthrowing Saddam Hussein and was hoping for a high-level position in whatever postwar government was set up in Iraq. Not to mention that he had a fraud conviction. Both the British intelligence service and the CIA had warned Wolfowitz and Feith not to rely on Chalabi.

Q. Is there a reason to do postwar planning if you aren't fairly well committed to starting a war?

A. I can't think of any.

Q. When was the next time Bush was briefed by Franks on the Iraq war plan?

A. On February 7.

Before that, on January 17 and February 1, Rumsfeld met with Franks and continued to press for a plan that could be implemented more quickly.

Then, on February 7, Franks presented a plan called "Generated Start" to Bush, Cheney, Rice, Powell, Rumsfeld, and others on the War Council. Franks told Bush the best months in which to invade Iraq were November to February because before and after those months, the temperature could easily be as high as 130 degrees, but Bush wanted to know if we could go earlier "if we had to."

Q. What did Franks say?

A. He said we could go, but it would be "ugly."

Q. On the afternoon of February 7, did the President's spokesperson, Ari Fleischer, make an announcement?

A. Yes. He announced that Cheney would be traveling to the Middle East at Bush's request on March 10.

GRAND JUROR: Had Bush already given his State of the Union speech address in which he said Iraq was part of the "Axis of Evil"?

A. Yes, but guess who's going to testify about that?

GRAND JURORS: Danny Crain.

Q. At this point, was the President consulting with or even officially informing Congress about his military activity and planning to invade Iraq?

A. Not to my knowledge. Senator Bob Graham, the Democrat who headed up the Senate Select Committee on Intelligence, first learned about plans and troop movements to Iraq from General Tommy Franks. In mid-February 2002, Franks had told him, kind of off the cuff, that they were going to be moving troops out of Afghanistan into Iraq.

Q. And that occurred in March, right?

A. Yes. In early March, approximately 1,800 United States troops, including the elite Fifth Group Special Forces who had been tracking Osama Bin Laden, were moved from Afghanistan to Iraq.

Q. You know what? We forgot to take a break.

FOREPERSON: No problem.

GRAND JUROR: We've lost all feeling in our legs, but we'll be fine.

Q. Good. See you all in fifteen.

•••

11:15 A.M.

ASSISTANT U.S. ATTORNEY: Agent Estrada, had the President also put the CIA to work in Iraq by March 2002?

A. Yes, he authorized the Central Intelligence Agency to provide weapons to the Kurds in the North, and the Shiites in the South. Basically, Bush wanted the CIA to use the ethnic and religious hostilities between those groups and Saddam Hussein's Sunni supporters to encourage Saddam's overthrow.

Q. When was the next time Bush and his War Council were briefed by Franks?

A. On February 28, Rumsfeld and Franks met to discuss the plan and possible bombing targets.

Then, on March 3, Franks gave another extensive briefing about the Iraq war plan to Bush, Rumsfeld, Powell, Cheney, and Rice.

Q. A week later, Cheney was off to the Middle East, correct? Where did he go?

A. He went to ten countries in ten days: Saudi Arabia, Qatar, Bahrain, Oman, Kuwait, Jordan, Turkey, the United Arab Emirates, Egypt, and Israel.

Q. What happened after Cheney got back?

A. One thing was that Cheney started making public appearances—

Q. Which was strange in and of itself.

A. True. He stepped up the rhetoric about a threat from Iraq and began implying again that there was a link between Saddam Hussein and al Qaeda. Also, the White

House announced, rather quietly, that Bush was going to France, Germany, and Russia in May.

Q. Back to the military planning, between March and mid-June 2002, how many major meetings did Franks have regarding the Iraq war plan that we know of?

A. At least six. One was March 29, with the Joint Chiefs of Staff. At that meeting, the military high command discussed a "Spike Plan," which involved aggressive air patrols and stepped-up air strikes to destabilize Iraq. Also, on April 11, Franks and Rumsfeld considered war preparations that would be relatively unobtrusive.

Q. How many more times did Franks meet with Bush and the War Council—including Rumsfeld, Cheney, Powell, and Rice—in April, May, and June?

A. Three times. They had one long briefing on April 20, a two-day one on May 10 and 11, and a third on June 19. By that time, Franks had developed two plans, "Generated Start" and "Running Start."

Q. Why a second plan?

A. Because Bush and Rumsfeld wanted one that was faster and more "agile"—fewer troops, more high tech. They were in a hurry. Cheney, according to Bob Woodward, was in a "frenzy" to invade Iraq.

Q. Special Agent Estrada, let's stop time for a moment, on June 19, 2002, the date that Franks brought Bush and the War Council the Running Start plan.

Based on available information, how many times did Franks meet with Rumsfeld about an Iraq war plan from November 21, 2001, through June 19, 2002?

A. At least thirteen.

Q. How many times did Franks meet with the Joint Chiefs to discuss the Iraq war plan during that period?

A. Several. I don't know the precise number.

Q. And how many top military officers were working with Franks on the plans?

A. I don't know, but he wasn't working on them by himself.

Q. How many iterations of the plans did Franks do, that you're aware of, by June 19?

A. At least five, but probably more.

Q. How many times do you know of that Franks discussed some version of the Iraq war plan at in-person briefings with Bush, Cheney, Powell, Rice, Rumsfeld, and the War Council during that period?

A. At least five.

Q. Was there additional military activity in the spring of 2002?

A. Yes, in May or June, the United States and Great Britain launched "Operation Southern Focus," which implemented the Spike Plan that the Joint Chiefs had discussed. As I mentioned, we had no authority to attack outside the no-fly zones, but Rumsfeld had simply changed the rules. Any bombings likely to cause more than thirty civilian deaths had to be approved by him personally.

Q. Do you know how many such bombings there were?

A. Rumsfeld approved at least fifty bombings that were likely to cause more than thirty civilian deaths before

March 19, 2003, the day Bush officially announced that we had invaded Iraq.

Q. Why did the President go to France, Germany, and Russia in May?

A. Germany was an important ally—although Bush isn't too thrilled with them right now, since they didn't go along with his plan for Iraq—and France and Russia are on the UN Security Council, whose support Bush wanted. We, China, and Great Britain are also on it.

Q. Shortly after Bush's return, in early June, Rumsfeld left for England and the Middle East, correct?

A. Yes. He met with British Defense Secretary Geoffrey Hoon in London first. And, as you'll hear tomorrow from Danny Crain, we were strategizing with the Brits to develop some credible justification for war. We were also conducting joint military operations.

After meeting with Hoon, Rumsfeld traveled to eight other countries, including Kuwait, Bahrain, and Qatar, where he spoke with troops already deployed there.

Q. What happened the day after the Running Start and Generated Start briefing?

A. The Navy began deploying aircraft carriers to the region around Iraq and not long afterwards, approximately 3,300 U.S. troops—plus munitions and equipment—were moved to al-Udeid Air Base in Qatar.

Q. Had Bush sought congressional approval for this military activity, or officially informed them of it?

A. No.

Q. But it is Congress' official government function to appropriate funds for military activity?

A. Yes.

Q. From what source were the funds for the operations against Iraq coming?

A. I don't know entirely, but I do know that in mid-July, Franks told Rumsfeld he needed approximately $700 million to preposition troops and supplies in Kuwait in preparation for an invasion of Iraq.

Q. Did he get the money?

A. Yes. On July 30, the President caused $700 million in Afghanistan war funds to be diverted to Iraq war preparations without first getting Congressional authorization or even advising them that he planned to do it.

Q. Do you know whether Bush ever discussed, with anyone, at any time, the *propriety* of invading Iraq—not just how to do it and how to get people to go along with it, but whether it was legally justified, or morally justified?

A. Yes, I do. He never had any such discussions with Cheney, Powell, Rice, Rumsfeld, or anyone else.

Q. How do you know that?

A. Bush himself said so. He told Bob Woodward that he "already knew" what the others thought.

Q. Have you prepared a summary of the Bush-Cheney administration's behind-the-scenes military activity against Iraq following the September 11 attacks through July 2002?

A. Yes, I have. It's no Venn diagram, but—

Q. You know about that?

A. Anyway, the chart is Exhibit 4:

Ex. 4

Unauthorized, Behind-the-Scenes Military Escalation against Iraq

September 17, 2001–July 30, 2002

Bush orders initial military planning against Iraq (Sept.)

Bush orders formal military attack plan for Iraq (Nov.)

Franks and Rumsfeld: thirteen meetings re: Iraq war plan

Franks: asked to do at least five revisions of Iraq plan; develops "Generated Start" and "Running Start"

Franks: meets with Joint Chiefs of Staff, discusses "Spike Plan" (March)

Bush, Cheney, Rice, Powell, Rumsfeld: five lengthy sessions on Iraq war plan with Franks, including briefings on detailed versions of "Generated Start" and "Running Start"

Defense Dept. (Rumsfeld, Wolfowitz, Feith): meetings with Ahmed Chalabi and INC Iraqi opposition

Bush: orders CIA to begin covert arming of Kurds & Shiites

Cheney: visits Saudi Arabia, Kuwait, Bahrain, Oman, United Arab Emirates, Jordan, Egypt, Israel, Qatar & Turkey (March)

Bush: visits France, Germany and Russia (May)
Rumsfeld: visits England, and eight other countries including Kuwait, Bahrain, and Qatar, where he spoke to United States troops already deployed there (June)
Rumsfeld: authorizes air strikes outside Iraq no-fly zone to "destabilize" Iraq; approves fifty strikes likely to kill thirty or more civilians (begins before June)
U.S.: moves Third Army HQ to Kuwait (Dec.);
moves Marine HQ to Bahrain (Feb.);
moves 1,800 troops to Iraq (March);
increases Air Strikes against Iraq, including more than 50 likely to kill 30 or more civilians;
deploys aircraft carriers to Gulf;
sends 3,300 troops and munitions to Qatar (June)
Bush: orders transfer of $700 million in Afghanistan war funds to Iraq military preparations (July 30)

Q. Okay. It's 12:30. How about an hour and fifteen minutes? You can spend some time looking at the chart and then have a long, lavish lunch with all the money you're making as grand jurors.

GRAND JUROR: Can we get snockered?

SECOND GRAND JUROR: Can we please vote him off?

•••

1:45 P.M.

ASSISTANT U.S. ATTORNEY: We're going to switch gears here for a bit.

Special Agent Estrada, when did the Bush-Cheney administration start referring to Afghanistan as "Phase One" in the "war on terror"?

A. Publicly? I believe that Press Secretary Ari Fleischer, the President, and Condoleezza Rice, at least, started publicly calling it Phase One as early as September 25, 2001.

Q. Now, if there's a Phase One, a reasonable inference would be that there's a Phase Two, correct?

A. Yes.

Q. But in September 2001, Bush et al. did not specifically say what Phase Two *was*, did they, at least not in public?

A. No, but behind the scenes they started calling Iraq Phase Two on September 17, 2001, the day Bush ordered preliminary military planning for an invasion of Iraq.

Q. Is it accurate then to say that from September 17 on, the defendants were engaged in a juggling act with regard to Iraq?

A. Yes, but it was not your run-of-the-mill tennis ball juggling act. It was more like a Penn and Teller performance where they were juggling all different things—knives, flaming torches, a couple of bowling pins, a Nerf ball, a clock, all in the air at once.

Q. Can you explain that?

A. Sure. The first problem was that they did not agree among themselves. Bush wanted to invade Iraq, but didn't think there was enough evidence. Rumsfeld wanted to invade Iraq ASAP. Cheney wanted to invade Iraq ASAP, but Bush had already said there wasn't enough evidence. Rice was in the same camp as Bush. Powell did not think we should invade Iraq, but believed that if we were going to do it, Bush needed to have domestic public support and to go through the UN process of obtaining a resolution.

The second problem was that they didn't have any intelligence that would justify an attack, and the British, in particular, were telling them that.

Third, they needed to make a *public* case to get international and domestic support, but the more they made their case publicly, the more people asked questions. The White House did not want to *answer* those questions because they were trying to conceal their military and planning activities.

Also, for some Americans, particularly Bush's base—his core constituents and the neocons—statements like "Saddam is a dire threat" created an expectation, not only that they would, but that they should, use military force immediately. That's the fourth problem.

The fifth was that to other people, those statements sounded like Bush et al. had already made up their minds to invade, without engaging in discussion or debate with Congress, and without seeking international support. Or, alternatively—problem six—the longer they went on saying Saddam was a threat without taking action, the more they undercut their argument that he *was* an urgent threat.

Number seven was that Bush wanted to, and, as you've now heard, *did* start military planning and escalation right away. Which is impossible to keep entirely secret and leads to the questions I just mentioned.

Finally, problem number eight was that Bush wanted to do all this in time for the 2002 congressional election. That's why they were juggling a clock.

On top of all that, the defendants had to juggle all of these considerations and constituencies while walking on a tightrope. They had to be careful not to offend or reveal too much to one audience while they were persuading, or concealing things, from another.

Q. And saying and doing different things depending on where you are and who you're with is pretty much the essence of fraud, isn't it?

A. Correct.

Q. Let's take an example: Germany, France, and Russia. What was Bush's situation when he went to those countries in May 2002?

A. It was a balancing act. Bush needed to convince the allies that Saddam was so dangerous that they had no choice but to join the United States in forcibly removing him. If was he was too aggressive, however, he risked revealing that he had already decided to invade. Bush's statements on May 23, 2002—after he met with German Chancellor Gerhardt Schroeder—illustrate the problem. In a joint press appearance, Schroeder said that Bush had assured him he had no concrete military plans to invade Iraq. Schroeder also declared that Germany was not prepared to use force.

And then Bush was asked this question:

> Mr. President, the Chancellor just said that your government does not seem to be very specific right now when it comes to plans to attack Iraq. Is that true, sir? And could you, nevertheless, try to explain to the German people what your goals are when it comes to Iraq?

Q. What did Bush say?

A. First, he said that Saddam was a serious threat:

> [T]he world knows my position about Saddam Hussein. He's a dangerous man. He's a dictator who gassed his own people. He's had a history of incredible human rights violations. And he is a—it's dangerous to think of a scenario in which a country like Iraq would team up with an al Qaeda type organization, particularly if and when they have the capacity, had the capacity, or when they have the capacity to deliver weapons of mass destruction via ballistic missile. And that's a threat. It's a threat to Germany, it's a threat to America, it's a threat to civilization itself.

And could I just say something about that part of Bush's answer in terms of fraud?

Q. Sure.

A. Well, this is like Bush's speech in May 2001, where he talked about Saddam and nuclear weapons, even though there was no evidence that Saddam had nuclear weapons then either. Bush makes several assertions that are true about Saddam's past behavior, and Saddam was, without question, a horrible person.

But then he starts talking about Saddam and al Qaeda and "when they had," or "when they have," the capacity to deliver WMD. At that point, he starts to stumble, as you can see. More important, though, he is no longer making an assertion. He is raising a kind of confused hypothetical.

Common sense tells you that the reason the President is not directly asserting a connection is that he knows what he's implying is not true. Bush has already been informed numerous times that Saddam and al Qaeda are not in cahoots and his use of the term "al Qaeda type" organization proves that he knows full well he cannot even honestly imply a link to al Qaeda. So he's bringing up a hypothetical that is entirely without basis and artfully worded to make all but the most careful listener believe that he, the President, is concerned about a link between Saddam Hussein and al Qaeda. Perhaps Bush may have thought he had plausible deniability because he merely sidled up to the edge of outright falsehood, but it is still fraud.

Q. What was the second part of the President's answer?

A. That the United States was going to consult with other countries. That was a theme the White House began to stress vis-à-vis the America public and Congress as well. They referred to it as "open dialogue":

> The Chancellor said that I promised consultations. I will say it again: I promise consultations with our close friend and ally. We will exert a uni-

> fied diplomatic pressure. We will share intelligence.

Q. What was his third point?

A. He said: "And I told the Chancellor that I have no war plans on my desk, which is the truth."

Q. *No war plans on my desk*. Does that remind anyone of someone we talked about before?

GRAND JURORS: Ken Lay.

Q. Exactly. You recall the example of a statement that was literally true—at least possibly—but definitely misleading? Lay was asked whether there was any truth to rumors about a takeover of Enron and he said "No." On cross-examination, however, he claimed he meant he didn't know of any *specific* company trying to take them over.

A. Could I make another point about Bush's statement, the part where he added, "which is the truth"?

Q. Please do.

A. Bush was vouching for his own honesty, in an aggressive way, to make people uncomfortable about questioning what he said, because people don't like to doubt the word of someone they trust. In a weird way, it makes them feel bad about themselves, as if they are being unfair or even rude.

Which is an odd consideration when you are talking about the reasons for war. What Bush did here is a very common technique used by people who are trying to deceive others.

Q. In fact, that was a technique Ken Lay used with stock analysts, wasn't it?

A. Yes, one allegation in the indictment against Lay was that in October of 2001, when there was growing public concern because Enron's stock had dropped 25 percent in a week, Lay had a telephone conference with some stock analysts.

The indictment also alleges that he prepared for the call in advance, as you would expect. When the analysts questioned Lay's response to their concerns, he made the following statements:

> [W]e're not trying to conceal anything. We're not hiding anything. . . .
>
> We're really trying to make sure that the analysts and shareholders and the debtholders really know what's going on here. So we are not trying to hold anything back. . . . I'm disclosing everything we've found.

Q. How does this example compare to Bush's statement that it was "the truth" that he had no war plans on his desk?

A. Well, just as Lay did, Bush had notice of the public's concerns and he knew that any public statement he made would be reported in the United States. Like Lay, of course, he also prepared his responses in advance.

Q. How do you know that?

A. Well, this president rarely speaks off the cuff but, more than that, his statement about having no war plans on his desk was clearly part of his preplanned talking points. Very deliberate. He said the same thing in France and Russia and even after he returned to the United States.

Here's what he said at the White House after meeting with the Australian Prime Minister John Howard, a month later, on June 13, 2002:

> I told the Prime Minister there are no war plans on my desk. I haven't changed my opinion about Saddam Hussein, however. He is—this is a person who gassed his own people, and possesses weapons of mass destruction. And so as I told the American people, and I told John, we'll use all tools at our disposal to deal with him. And, of course, before there is any action—military action, I would closely consult with our close friend. There are no plans on my desk right now.

GRAND JUROR: How is that not just a lie? Bush was trying to make people think he had no plans to go to war, when he had already done all that stuff we just heard.

Q. Did other Bush administration spokespersons also say he had no war plans on his desk during that period?

A. Yes, they all said Bush had made "no decision" on war, even up to the last few days before the invasion, but on July 15, 2002, on Ted Koppel's *Nightline*, Powell said:

> What we have consistently said is that the President has no plan on his desk to invade Iraq at the moment, nor has one been presented to him,

> nor have his advisors come together to put a plan to him.

Q. Jurors, I'm not sure if I've explained this point yet, but you should be aware that the law holds a person responsible for the acts of his subordinates when those acts are done at his direction, so, legally speaking, Powell's statement is the President's statement. However, the Bush administration has made it clear as well that the President's cabinet members and press spokespersons are speaking for him, correct?

A. Yes, both Press Secretary Ari Fleischer and his successor, Scott McClellan, have emphasized that when they were speaking it was the equivalent of the President speaking. They have also stressed that Bush's advisers speak with one voice, and that voice is the President's. For example, on September 3 2002, Ari Fleischer was bombarded with questions about an apparent internal White House struggle regarding Iraq that had reared its ugly head in late August. The Vice President and Secretary of State Powell appeared to be publicly contradicting each other on whether the administration should work with the United Nations or simply march to war on its own, so one reporter asked:

> Q. I'm wondering . . . who does the President himself look to, to speak for the administration on matters of foreign policy?
>
> MR. FLEISHER: Himself. The President will speak when he thinks the time is appropriate. If he has

> something to share, he will do so, of course, as he always has done.
>
> But the President has one of the most experienced, wise teams surrounding him, when it comes to defense and foreign policy, of any administration ever assembled. He has a superb team, and each and every one of them is capable of speaking out repeatedly, and they will.
>
> Q. So, does that mean that when we hear Dick Cheney speak, or Don Rumsfeld or some of these others, that we should view this as part of a mix of discussions, and that the definitive word is going to come from the President himself?
>
> MR. FLEISCHER: Well, I think you're hearing the same message from all of them. As you know, they meet very often through the National Security Council and through other mechanisms, and so they all hear the same conversations, understand what the President's direction is. And then their job is to go out and share that presidential reflection. Secretary Rumsfeld, as you know, is briefing today.

Q. Besides establishing that the President's senior officials are speaking at his direction, does Fleischer's statement have additional significance in terms of this case?

A. Yes, it does. Fleischer was explicitly stating the obvious fact that the President, the Vice President, the National Security Adviser, and Secretaries of Defense and State all meet frequently together, as well as that they intentionally agree upon the "same message." Therefore, the defendants' statements about prewar intelligence were the product of concerted action in pursuit of a mutually agreed-upon goal; in other words, a conspiracy.

Q. Wouldn't we expect the President and his advisors to work together toward a certain goal?

A. Yes, the conspiracy to defraud arises from their agreement to convey a unified public message that was deliberately misleading.

Q. In addition to vouching for the President's honesty, did White House officials also affirmatively vouch for the *accuracy* of the President's representations and those of his spokespersons?

A. Yes, one instance of that was when *Washington Post* reporter Dana Millbank asked Fleischer about false statements that the President had been making for an article Millbank subsequently wrote called, "For President, Facts are Malleable" and Fleischer said, "The President's statements are well documented and supported by the facts. We reject any allegation to the contrary."

Q. Would it have been important for the American people and Congress to know the true extent of military action and planning for war against Iraq that the defendants had already undertaken by the end of July 2002?

A. Absolutely. They were entitled to honest information. Maybe not all the details, but an honest presentation of the White House's real arguments for why we should even be thinking about invading Iraq. Americans and Congress were also entitled to know the true extent of the military planning and activity—and government expenditures for war—that had already occurred long before the President started the "open dialogue" in September 2002.

Q. The administration was carrying on extensive behind-the-scenes preparation for war in other spheres, too, wasn't it?

A. Yes. I'll leave that to—

Q. Special Agent Crain. You'll finally get to meet him tomorrow.

A. Tell him you've heard he was the Kalamazoo High School Arm Wrestling Champion of 1983 . . .

Q. Thank you for your testimony, Agent Estrada. See you all tomorrow.

END OF DAY FOUR

UNITED STATES v. GEORGE W. BUSH et al. GRAND JURY PRESENTATION

Testimony of FBI Special Agent Daniel Crain

9:00 A.M.

ASSISTANT U.S. ATTORNEY: Good morning, everybody. Any questions before we bring in our witness?

GRAND JUROR: Are we going to say something about the arm wrestling?

Q. How about this afternoon? Could somebody please see if he's out there? [Whereupon the witness enters and is sworn]

Q. Special Agent—

A. Supervisory Special Agent.

Q. Okay . . . And what is your name?

A. My name is Daniel NMN Crain.

Q. NMN?

A. No middle name. Just Danny Crain.

Q. And what do you do?

A. I am a Supervisory Special Agent with the Office of Export Enforcement within the Department of Commerce.

Q. Okay. What does that mean?

A. It means that I investigate export violations, especially ones that relate to items usable for nuclear proliferation and nuclear weapons purposes.

Q. Is that the topic of your testimony today?

A. No, I'm on loan to the Joint Task Force that's investigating the President's possible conspiracy to defraud the United States in regards to prewar intelligence.

I'm in charge of it.

Q. Could you please tell us, briefly, about your educational background and how you ended up as a Special Agent with the Department of Commerce?

A. Yes, ma'am. I graduated from Kalamazoo High School and went to Michigan on a full basketball scholarship—not to toot my own horn.

Q. Of course not. University of Michigan?

GRAND JUROR: Go blue.

A. Exactly. I was also the arm wrestling champion of Kalamazoo High in 1983.

Q. We heard.

A. I know. Agent Estrada, right? I never should have told him that.

Anyway, I started out in industrial engineering at Michigan. But I decided to switch to business, and I was recruited by the Commerce Department during my senior year.

Q. What kind of cases do you usually work on?

A. Anything involving illegal exports of equipment or technology to countries that are restricted, like China or Iraq or Iran.

Q. In this case, you are not testifying as an expert, right, you're testifying as investigator?

A. The lead investigator. Yes, ma'am.

Q. Okay, you are going to have to stop calling me ma'am . . .

A. Yes, ma'am . . . Sorry . . .

Q. What part of this case have you worked on?

A. The whole thing. But I understand Campbell and Estrada have testified up through topic three on Exhibit 1, so you probably want to ask me about the Downing Street Memos.

Q. Oh, well, thank you.

Before we turn to those, though, as of March 2002, were our allies buying the administration's arguments about Iraq?

A. For the most part, no. And the administration was not happy about it.

For example, on March 11, when Rice appeared on the PBS *News Hour*, Jim Lehrer asked her:

> Is it fair to say, Dr. Rice, that all of our major allies—at least those who have spoken publicly, with a couple of exceptions—have come out loud and clear against military action against Iraq?

Q. How did Rice respond?

A. She bristled, insisting that our major allies had not said they were "unequivocally opposed to any particular action against Iraq." She wanted "to be very clear," she said, "that the United States has not said that the time has come for the use of force against Iraq. We're in a phase of consulting with our friends and allies."

Q. Relative to Great Britain, what did this "consulting" phase consist of?

A. It was not a consultation as to *whether* we should or should not invade Iraq, nor was it a consultation about whether it was *legal* to invade, but rather how we could manipulate the situation so we *could* invade. With France, Germany, Russia, and China, among others, it was as if Bush alone was performing the juggling act Agent Estrada talked about and they were the audience. But with Prime Minister Tony Blair, it was as if they were juggling partners. The British and American public, Parliament, Congress, and much of the rest of the world and its leaders were the audience.

Q. In fact, Bush had been fairly direct with Blair about his intention to invade Iraq from late September 2001 on, hadn't he?

A. Yes. According to Woodward's *Plan of Attack*, as early as September 20, 2001, Bush told Blair he planned to "come back" to Iraq after invading Afghanistan.

Q. How do you know what people in the Bush-Cheney administration were saying to the British, and vice versa?

A. There are many public accounts, public statements, and news articles from that time frame, but perhaps the most vivid evidence is in the Downing Street Memos I mentioned.

Q. Which you thought I should ask you about before?

A. I still do, but I think we should look at Exhibit 5 first, which is just a barebones timeline that will put the Downing Street Memos in context:

Ex. 5
Iraq War Timeline (short version)

Sept. 4, 2002	Bush announces he will seek congressional vote on Iraq and begin "open dialogue."
Oct. 16, 2002	Congress passes Authorization to Use Military Force Against Iraq.
Nov. 8, 2002	The UN passes Resolution 1441 that requires Iraq to submit to enhanced inspections. It does not authorize the use of force.
Nov. 18, 2002	UN inspectors arrive in Iraq.
Mar. 17, 2003	Bush gives Saddam Hussein an ultimatum to leave Iraq within 48 hours; UN Secretary General Kofi Annan instructs the UN inspectors to leave.
Mar. 19, 2003	Bush makes official announcement that we have invaded Iraq.
May 1, 2003	Bush announces end of major combat operations in Iraq.

Q. The Downing Street Memos memorialize meetings and conversations that occurred before the President announced he was beginning a dialogue about Iraq in September, correct?

A. Yes. There were six of them, from March of 2002 and one dated July 23, 2002. They were leaked by FNU LNU—

Q. Maybe you should tell the jurors what FNU LNU stands for.

A. First Name Unknown, Last Name Unknown. We don't know who leaked the memo, but it was published on May 1, 2005, in the *London Sunday Times*, precisely two years after Bush announced the end of major combat operations. That was the time he flew onto the deck of the USS *Abraham Lincoln* off the coast of San Diego and spoke to the country while he was standing under the "Mission Accomplished" banner. On that day, by the way, the President declared that the battle of Iraq had "removed an ally of al Qaeda," which was yet another attempt to mislead Americans about the nonexistent connection between Saddam's regime and al Qaeda.

It just occurred to me, though, that we need to take a break so I can move my OGV.

Q. OGV?

A. Official Government Vehicle. I'll be back at eleven o'clock sharp.

Q. Well, jurors, I guess we might as well take a break too. See you all at eleven. Sharp.

•••

11:00 A.M. SHARP

ASSISTANT U.S. ATTORNEY: Everyone has made it safely

back, I see, including our witness. Agent Crain, what is Downing Street?

A. Downing Street is a reference to Number 10 Downing Street, the official residence and offices of British Prime Minister Tony Blair. It's similar to the White House.

Q. How do we know—

A. That the memos are real? On June 6, 2005, Bush and Blair were asked this question about the first one that was leaked:

> On Iraq, the so-called Downing Street memo from July 2002 says intelligence and facts were being fixed around the policy of removing Saddam through military action. Is this an accurate reflection of what happened? Could both of you respond?

Q. What did Prime Minister Blair say?

A. He said:

> No, the facts were not being fixed in any shape or form at all. And let me remind you that that memorandum was written before we then went to the United Nations. . . . And the fact is we decided to go to the United Nations and went through that process, which resulted in the November 2002 United Nations resolution, to give a final chance to Saddam Hussein to comply with international law. He didn't do so. And that was the reason why we had to take military action.

Q. What did President Bush say?

A. The President's answer was extremely interesting. He used the same MO he and his aides had used in response to Clarke and O'Neill: shoot the messenger. In this instance, though, it was not so much shoot the messenger as take a sideswipe at him.

Bush first mentioned that the memo had been dropped "out in the middle of his race," referring to Blair's reelection campaign, as if to suggest the timing of its appearance made it less worthy of consideration. As you'll soon hear, however, that implication was unwarranted, because the memo had been written in July of 2002.

Then Bush disparaged the memo by suggesting it was merely the opinion of "*somebody* [who] said, well, you know, we had made up our mind to go to use military force to deal with Saddam." Insinuating that the memo was insignificant because it was the opinion of "somebody"—in other words, some unreliable nutcase—was also deliberately deceptive, because as the President well knew, and I'll explain in a moment, the "somebody" whose comments were recounted was Sir Richard Dearlove, the head of British intelligence. Not exactly just "somebody."

Finally, the President followed Blair's lead by claiming that the two of them had not made up their minds in July; they had gone to the UN in September, and it was Saddam's fault that we had to invade his country—an obvious nonanswer to the question of whether they had used the UN process as a sham.

What Bush and Blair were counting on was that most of

their constituents had no idea what the Downing Street Memos actually said, and astounding as it may be, most people still don't.

Q. How do the Downing Street Memos fit into this investigation?

A. The case for fraud does not depend on them. We could ignore them entirely, and there would still be ample evidence of fraud, nor are the Downing Street Memos "smoking guns." There are almost never smoking guns—even in cases where there are guns—but they are a very important category of evidence. They flesh out the defendants' behind-the-scenes negotiations and military planning, but they also work the opposite way: Details which we can already prove confirm the reliability of the Downing Street memos.

Q. In this memo there *are* a striking number of details that are corroborated by other evidence in the case, aren't there?

A. Yes, there are. The same is true of the six additional Downing Street memos from March 2002 that were leaked to the British press in mid-June of 2005.

Q. Let's turn then to Exhibit 6. What is that?

A. Exhibit 6 is the heading portion of the memo:

Ex. 6
Heading of July 23, 2002, Downing St. Memo

SECRET AND STRICTLY PERSONAL—
UK EYES ONLY

DAVID MANNING
From: Matthew Rycroft
Date: 23 July 2002
S 195/02
cc: Defence Secretary, Foreign Secretary, Attorney General, Sir Richard Wilson, John Scarlett, Francis Richards, CDS, C, Jonathan Powell, Sally Morgan, Alastair Campbell
IRAQ: PRIME MINISTER'S MEETING, 23 JULY

Q. Who is David Manning?

A. Manning's title is Foreign Policy Secretary, a rough equivalent of Rice's position at that time, National Security Adviser. Matthew Rycroft is an aide to Manning who took the minutes of the meeting.

Q. The memo starts off by stating that the "copy addresses"—all the names mentioned—"and you," meaning Manning, met the Prime Minister on July 23 to discuss Iraq. Who was listed as having been copied on the memo?

A. Excluding Rycroft, all of the people who attended the meeting, as well as their titles, are listed in Exhibit 7:

Ex. 7
Participants in July 23, 2003, Downing St. Meeting

Tony Blair	Prime Minister
David Manning	Foreign Policy Secretary
Geoffrey Hoon	Defence Secretary
Jack Straw	Foreign Secretary
Lord Goldsmith	Attorney-General
Sir Richard Wilson	Cabinet Secretary
John Scarlett	Chair, Joint Intel Committee
Francis Richards	Director, Government Communications
CDS/Sir Michael Boyce	Chief of Defense Staff
C/Sir Richard Dearlove	Chair, Joint Intelligence Committee
Jonathan Powell	Chief of Staff
Sally Morgan	Director, Political and Government Relations
Alastair Campbell	Director of Communications & Strategy

Q. We're not going to go over each paragraph, but what does the first paragraph say?

A. I have that set out in Exhibit 8:

Ex. 8
July 23, 2002, Downing St. Memo (Dearlove)

C reported on his recent talks in Washington. There was a perceptible shift in attitude. Military

> action was now seen as inevitable. Bush wanted to remove Saddam, through military action, justified by the conjunction of terrorism and WMD. But the intelligence and facts were being fixed around the policy. The NSC had no patience with the UN route, and no enthusiasm for publishing material on the Iraqi regime's record. There was little discussion in Washington of the aftermath after military action.

Q. Who is "C"?

A. C is Sir Richard Dearlove, the head of British intelligence, or MI6. And his "recent talks in Washington" were with his American counterpart, CIA Director George Tenet, and most likely others as well.

Q. Essentially, based on the conversations he had, Dearlove was advising Blair and Blair's senior policy advisers that military action was seen as inevitable in the United States?

A. Yes. Dearlove was also saying that intelligence was "being fixed around the policy."

Q. Was that an important revelation?

A. Absolutely, because there was considerable skepticism, both before and after the war, about the sincerity of the President's claim that no decision had been made to use force. On March 13, 2003, for example, Helen Thomas asked Presidential Press Secretary Ari Fleischer, "Why is the President going through this charade of diplomacy when he so obviously wants to go to war?" So it was a sensitive issue, to put it mildly.

Q. You told us about Bush's response to the memo in June of 2005. What was the White House's response when the July 23 Downing Street Memo was initially published in early May?

A. The first White House response was not until May 16, when Bush's new spokesperson, Scott McClellan, was asked about it. He did not deny the memo's authenticity but said, nevertheless, that it was "flat-out wrong" to say that intelligence was "being fixed around the policy."

GRAND JUROR: How did McClellan respond to the details in the memo?

A. He said he hadn't read it. He then said something that you'll find quite familiar; that the President "in a very public way, [had] reached out to people across the world, went to the United Nations and tried to resolve this in a diplomatic manner." Saddam Hussein, McClellan claimed, was the one, in the end, who chose continued defiance. And only then was the decision made, as a last resort, to go into Iraq.

It was exactly the same answer that the President and Prime Minister Blair gave in June.

Q. Was there a major flaw in that answer?

A. It wasn't true.

Q. Besides that?

A. The public outreach that McClellan was talking about was a component of the marketing campaign that occurred after the July 23 meeting. And the question that the Downing Street Memo revived was the same one that

Helen Thomas had asked: *Was the diplomacy that started in September a charade*? In other words, had the President decided to go to war before the maneuvering ever began? McClellan was relying on the very process that was in doubt to prove that the process was valid.

Q. Let's go have some lunch . . .

•••

1:00 P.M.

ASSISTANT U.S. ATTORNEY: How is everyone doing?

Let's focus back on Exhibit 8, "for the nonce," as one of my favorite judges used to say. Based on the first paragraph of the Downing Street Memo that's reproduced there, we know that Richard Dearlove, also known as "C," reported to Blair that the prevailing attitude in Washington in mid-July 2002 was that military action against Iraq was inevitable. We also know—it's undisputed—that the memo is an authentic and accurate account of the meeting.

Given those facts, Special Agent Crain, what is the one question that remains regarding the reliability of Dearlove's report on his talks in Washington?

A. The only question is whether Dearlove was a reliable observer and evaluator of the Bush administration's attitude towards military action against Iraq at the time.

Q. Based on what you know about Dearlove and his role in gathering and presenting preinvasion intelligence, would you consider him a credible and reliable witness on this issue?

A. Yes. First of all, he was a direct participant in the talks he was recounting, so he had an excellent opportunity to observe. Second, Dearlove is a highly intelligent, well-educated man, who had worked for the British Secret Intelligence Service for thirty-six years. Clearly, he was a capable evaluator of that type of situation.

Related to that, by the summer of 2002, both the British and American intelligence services were actively preparing a "case" for war that could be presented to the public, so Dearlove was in an excellent position to know that intelligence was being "fixed around the policy."

GRAND JUROR: What does that mean, intelligence being "fixed around the policy"?

Q. Let's come back to that, okay?

A. So, then, we would ask: Would a person in Dearlove's position have a motive to lie about the U.S. stance on the war as of July 23, 2002? Of course not. He knew Blair was relying on the accuracy of his input to gauge how to deal with President Bush and to make important decisions about Iraq.

Q. Did Dearlove, *in particular*, have reason to lie about his talks with Bush's senior policy advisers in Washington?

A. No. For one thing, there is no indication that Dearlove or anyone else at the July 23 Downing Street meeting was particularly exercised about the idea that the U.S. was fixing the intelligence to make its case for war. Dearlove himself is an advocate of spreading democracy through military intervention, so—

Q. How do you know that?

A. Dearlove is a member of the Henry Jackson Society, and that's their overriding principle. Bush's former Defense Board Chair, Richard Perle, supports that group.

Q. Remember him, jurors? A proponent of the PNAC principles?

GRAND JURORS: [nod heads vigorously]

A. Apparently, Agent Campbell nailed that point. Back to Dearlove. From the account in Rycroft's memo, it appears that no one at the meeting was shocked to hear that the Bush-Cheney administration had decided to invade Iraq despite the lack of any intelligence to warrant it. The British were *not* alarmed or surprised by news that military action was inevitable, because it was not news to them. The British had already known for months that Bush had decided to go to war.

Q. In fact, others at the meeting acknowledged that U.S. military action was inevitable, didn't they?

A. Yes. Jack Straw, the Foreign Secretary, said that "it seemed clear that Bush had made up his mind to take military action, even if the timing was not yet decided."

Q. Of course, Defence—that's "ence," British spelling.

COURT REPORTER: Thank you. My transcription program will change it anyway.

Q. Defense Secretary Geoffrey Hoon also knew about U.S. plans for military action, didn't he?

A. Yes, we know that he and Defense Secretary Rumsfeld were in communication and Hoon's statements on July 23 reflect inside knowledge of U.S. plans and activities. Hoon said, for example, that the U.S. had already begun "spikes of activity" to put pressure on Saddam's regime.

Q. That was almost exactly the term the Joint Chiefs had used to describe the increased number of air strikes, wasn't it?

A. Yes. They called it the Spike Plan. We also know that the RAF, the Royal Air Force, was participating in the escalating air campaign by July 2002.

Q. Defense Secretary Hoon was aware of the U.S. timetable for war as well?

A. Yes, he reported that no decisions had been made, but "the most likely timing in U.S. minds for military action to begin was January, with the timeline beginning thirty days before the U.S. congressional elections."

GRAND JUROR: Are you saying that the timing of the war, or at least the "public outreach" to get support for it, was tied to the 2002 elections?

Q. That will be up to you to decide, but we'll have more evidence about it later.

In the meantime, just so everyone knows, the 2002 congressional elections were scheduled in November, as you can see from Exhibit 8—just two months after the President's September 4th announcement that he would be seeking congressional authorization to use force.

A. May I interject for a moment?

Q. Absolutely.

A. Bush did not, on September 4, actually announce that he was seeking an authorization to use force. The White

House staged a photo session of Bush meeting with congressional leaders of both parties. After that, Bush told the press that he had been discussing the serious threat posed by Saddam Hussein with this bipartisan group. Then he said, "At the appropriate time, this administration will go to the Congress to seek approval for—necessary to deal with the threat." That is an exact quote as it appears on the White House website. Nothing omitted.

Bush literally stopped short of announcing that he was asking Congress for an authorization to use force, and common sense tells you why: If he had said he wanted to use force, he would have been contradicting his "open dialogue" theme. Within less than three weeks, however, the President submitted a draft resolution that proposed that very thing. Then, on October 16, just three weeks before the congressional election—and barely six weeks after Bush's photo op—Congress passed the Joint Resolution to Authorize Use of Military Force.

Q. Back to the July 23, 2002, Downing Street meeting. Did anyone else there have inside information about U.S. military plans?

A. Yes, Chief Defense Secretary Michael Boyle informed the group that the U.S. military had two plans, Generated Start and Running Start, which was correct, of course. He also said that military planners "would brief CENTCOM on 1–2 August, Rumsfeld on 3 August and Bush on 4 August." Based on numerous sources, including Bob Woodward's book *Plan of Attack*, we know that was true as well, though possibly off by a day or two.

Q. And CENTCOM is U.S. Central Command, the headquarters of our top military leaders in the Middle East?

A. Yes.

Q. Did Prime Minister Blair or anyone else at the July 23 meeting express any concerns about President Bush's strategy?

A. Yes. They were concerned that there was no factual basis to support a case for war. After commenting that he, too, thought Bush had made up his mind to invade Iraq, Foreign Secretary Straw added that "the case was thin. Saddam was not threatening his neighbours, and his WMD capability was less than that of Libya, North Korea or Iran."

The lack of factual justification created a second concern: no *legal* justification. Lord Goldsmith, the Attorney General, advised that desire for regime change was not a legal basis for military action, and in this case, neither was self-defense or humanitarian intervention.

Q. Knowing there was neither a factual nor a legal justification for war, did Prime Minister Blair and his senior aides decide not to support the U.S. plan for military action against Iraq?

A. No.

Q. What did they conclude?

A. Well, several, including Dearlove and Blair, noted that the United States did not want to take the time to go through the UN and get its mandate for war, but the British very much wanted the U.S. to do just that. They concluded that they should work with the Bush administration to devise an ultimatum that would require Saddam

Hussein to readmit the UN weapons inspectors. This is how Matthew Rycroft put it:

> The Prime Minister said that it would make a big difference politically and legally if Saddam refused to allow in the UN inspectors. Regime change and WMD were linked in the sense that it was the regime that was producing the WMD.

Q. What was the bottom line? Did they have some action items?

A. Yes, they did. They acknowledged that they disagreed with the Bush administration on the political strategy needed to lay the groundwork for the war, and they agreed that "despite US resistance, [they] should explore discreetly the ultimatum." As the memo also noted, "It would be important for the Prime Minister to set out the political context to Bush." And Foreign Secretary Straw said that he was going to talk about it with Colin Powell.

Q. Did the July discussion between the U.S. and Britain differ significantly from the talks they were having in March of 2002, when Condoleezza Rice was insisting that the President had made no decision about Iraq and that we were consulting with our friends and allies?

A. No, ma'am.

Q. How do you know that?

A. From the six March 2002 Downing Street Memos that were leaked to and published in the British press in mid-June of 2005.

Q. And are those memos of unquestioned authenticity, just as the July 23 memo was?

A. Yes.

Q. What do they show?

A. Overall, the memos show that Blair's advisers told him in March 2002 that the U.S. position toward Iraq was baseless and legally unjustifiable. They thought Saddam Hussein might have some chemical or biological weapons, but even on that point, their evidence was weak.

They had no evidence whatsoever that Saddam had nuclear weapons, and only slight evidence that he even had any continuing nuclear-weapons programs. The British noted that Saddam had used WMD in the past—a reference to his use of deadly mustard gas killing Iranian troops during the Iran-Iraq war, as well as thousands of Kurds in Northern Iraq in 1987 and 1988—and "could do so again if his regime were threatened." However, they stated, "there is no greater threat now than in recent years that Saddam will use WMD."

The memos also demonstrate that, as early as March 2002, there was considerable communication between senior British and American foreign policy advisers, including between President Bush and Prime Minister Blair, regarding how to start a war against Iraq. Remember the December 1997 *Weekly Standard* article that Wolfowitz and our Ambassador to Iraq Zalmay Khalilzad wrote: "How to Remove Saddam: A How-to Guide"? That title would describe the discussion between the British and the Americans that was occurring in March. And July. And September. Right up until the invasion.

Q. Do you have some examples of their conversations in March?

A. Yes, I do. On March 12, 2002, Condoleezza Rice's counterpart, David Manning, told her that to get British support, the U.S. would need to demonstrate concern for world opinion and "the insistence of many countries on the need for a legal base" for an invasion. Manning said that a new refusal by Saddam to accept "unfettered inspections would be a powerful argument" that they could use to persuade the international community.

Here is how Ambassador Christopher Meyer explained it to Deputy Secretary Paul Wolfowitz on March 17, 2002: The British would back the U.S. in pursuing "regime change" in Iraq, but it would be a "tough sell" domestically and in Europe. So Meyer suggested that the two countries "wrongfoot" Saddam on the inspectors and the UN Security Council Resolution.

Q. Meaning what?

A. Meaning to follow the UN process and hope that Saddam tripped himself up. That was the only decision that Bush had not made as of March 2002. He had not decided whether to join the Brits' "staged approach" involving the U.N., or to just attack Iraq unilaterally, with or without a resolution or a coalition.

To wrongfoot or not to wrongfoot: That was the only question Bush ever had about invading Iraq.

Q. Let's take a break.

•••

3:15 P.M.

ASSISTANT U.S. ATTORNEY: Is it my imagination, or are we missing two people?

GRAND JUROR: They went to Starbucks. Coffee downstairs gets old after a while.

Q. I hate to tell you this, but nobody who works in this building is brave enough to drink that coffee.

GRAND JUROR: *Now* she tells us.

Q. Our missing jurors back now? Great.

Special Agent Crain, you mentioned that Bush's opening act in the prewar production was his photo opportunity with bipartisan leaders on September 4, 2002?

A. That's correct. It was quite remarkable.

Within precisely seven minutes, Bush fired out his messages, over and over—like a pitching machine. He said at least seven times that Saddam Hussein was a "serious threat" or "threat." He said that "doing nothing was not an option."

But his main theme was this: he looked forward, he insisted, "to an open dialogue with Congress and the American people about the threat." The President used some variation of that statement at least seven times as well. His administration was going to "fully participate" in congressional hearings. He was going to "work with our friends in the world." In fact, Prime Minister Blair was coming that very weekend, Canadian Prime Minister Jean Chrétien on

Monday, and Bush was going to talk with the leaders of China, France, and Russia by phone in a few days.

In case anyone missed it, Bush said it again: he was "starting an open dialogue with elected officials and, therefore, the American people, about our future and how best to deal with it."

Then he said it again: he and the bipartisan leaders "were all good people sitting around the table talking about how best to secure the homeland." After that, Bush nodded toward the Democrats and Republicans who had just been sitting around opening that dialogue with him. It was like the defendant who tries to prove he hadn't robbed a bank by insisting that he had spent the day of the robbery lying around on the couch. Then, by way of proof, he points to it and says, "If you don't believe me, there is the *very* couch that I was lying on."

It's important to note here, though, that Bush was not merely stressing his cooperative approach to the issue of Iraq. He was also emphasizing that he hadn't decided what to do about it yet. Implying that he was still a blank slate on the issue of Iraq, open to ideas from the public, from allies, and Congress, he consistently referred to the *threat* as immediate, but always referred to his *response* to the threat as unknown and in the future.

Q. What happened the next day?

A. On September 5, 2002, approximately one hundred United States and British planes dropped precision-guided munitions onto Saddam Hussein's major air-defense facility to prepare the way for U.S. Special Forces helicopters from Jordan to enter Iraqi air space. They used at least seven types of aircraft, including U.S. F-15 Strike Eagles and Royal Air Force Tornado ground-attack planes.

Q. In the course of this investigation, has a man named Tim Goodrich been interviewed?

A. Yes, he has.

Q. Who is he?

A. He is a twenty-five-year-old man who joined the U.S. Air Force at the age of eighteen, after dreaming about joining the military since he was a child. He was honorably discharged in 2003 and later cofounded Iraq Veterans Against the War.

Q. Was he in the U.S. Air Force on September 5, 2002?

A. Yes, he was. He was stationed in the Persian Gulf working as an electronics technician in aircraft tech support.

Q. Did he hear President Bush's statements about diplomacy and open dialogue in early September 2002?

A. Yes, and he was outraged by them.

Q. Why?

A. Because he was personally involved in tech support for the planes that were flying out to strike Iraq's air-defense facility. This is what Tim Goodrich said: "We were dropping bombs then, and I saw bombing intensify . . . All the documents coming out now, the Downing Street memo and others, confirm what I had witnessed in Iraq. The war had already begun while our leaders were telling us that they were going to try all diplomatic options first." In fact, Goodrich said, while Bush was saying we were going to try diplomacy, "we were over there bombing the heck out of them."

Q. By September 12, 2002, what was the status of the United States military buildup in the area around Iraq?

A. Well, in the first few days of August, as Defense Secretary Hoon mentioned at the July 23 Downing Street meeting, Franks had met with his commanders regarding the Running Start plan. They had finally decided on the Hybrid Plan, which incorporated features of both Generated Start and Running Start. Franks told the commanders to be ready to invade immediately.

On August 5, 2002, Franks briefed Bush, Cheney, Rice, Rumsfeld, Powell, and others on the Hybrid Plan. Not long after that, Franks informed his commanders that they would be using the Hybrid Plan in preparing to invade Iraq.

By September 12, the United States had already moved 40,000 military personnel and over 350,000 tons of equipment—including battle tanks, Bradley fighting vehicles, Multiple Launch Rocket Systems, armored command vehicles, bulldozers, trucks, and Humvees—to areas around Iraq.

Q. But that was not all, was it?

A. No, at the risk of sounding like Dr. Seuss, that was not all. Bush and his team were, as Dearlove had put it, "fixing intelligence around the policy," and getting ready to serve it. They had put out appetizers, but the big spread would not be laid out until September.

Q. Okay. We'll see you all tomorrow. Have a nice evening!

•••

END OF DAY FIVE

UNITED STATES v. GEORGE W. BUSH et al. GRAND JURY PRESENTATION

Testimony of FBI Special Agent
Daniel Crain

9:00 A.M.

ASSISTANT U.S. ATTORNEY: Good morning. We're ready for Agent Crain. Could someone please go get him? [Whereupon the witness enters the room and is sworn]

Q. Good morning. Special Agent Crain, the jurors have now heard detailed testimony about the defendants' behind-the-scenes planning for war, military escalation, and strategizing with the British about how to sell the war to the public and our allies. Do we have a way of knowing what intelligence information was available to the President when he set this leviathan in motion?

A. Yes, we do. The Senate Select Committee on Intelligence, which was a bipartisan committee, has analyzed the intelligence-community assessments relating to Iraq that were in effect at various times before the President started pushing for the war. They issued factual findings and conclusions in a lengthy report that was published on July 7, 2004.

Q. Okay. We're going to call that the Senate Report. Is it fair to say that a key focus of that report was the status of prewar intelligence on the issue of weapons of mass destruction?

A. Yes, it is. Weapons of mass destruction, or WMD, is a term that is commonly used to refer to chemical, biological, and nuclear weapons, but nuclear weapons are considered to be of greatest concern for national-security purposes.

It's important to note that the defendants frequently used the term WMD in a misleading fashion. They would say, in so many words, *We know Saddam Hussein has WMD because he used them in the past.* That was literally true, but deceptive, because Saddam Hussein did use poisonous gas against the Kurds and Iranians in the 1990s, but he has never had nuclear weapons.

Q. Did the Senate Committee analyze the three types of weapons as a group?

A. No, they did a separate analysis for each category.

Q. Jurors, just so you know, we are going to concentrate only on the nuclear-weapons issue in this presentation. Agent Crain, what does the term "intelligence community" refer to?

A. The intelligence community, or IC, is comprised of the intelligence branches of the Departments of State, Energy, and Defense, the National Security Agency, and others. Most intelligence assessments are prepared under the direction of the CIA—the Central Intelligence Agency—but information supplied by all of the agencies is considered in compiling the final product. Dissenting opinions, which are not uncommon, are included either in the text or in footnotes.

Intelligence assessments have different names. The

most comprehensive ones, those that evaluate all potential security risks posed by a specific country, are called National Intelligence Estimates, or NIEs. They usually take six months or more to prepare. Others are more focused and have different names and abbreviations, all of which contribute to the rich alphabet soup of government-speak.

Q. Based on the Senate Report, what can you tell us about the IC's assessment of Iraq's nuclear weapons capability as of November 21, 2001?

A. The most recent assessment available on that date was an ICA—Intelligence Community Assessment—called "Iraq: Steadily Pursuing WMD Capabilities" that was published in December 2000, a report about Iraq's possible chemical, biological, or nuclear weapons. The IC had been asked to assess the status of Iraq's WMD efforts since the departure of UNSCOM in 1998.

Q. Okay. What is UNSCOM, and please explain what departure you're talking about.

A. UNSCOM is the acronym for the United Nations weapons inspection team, or the UN Special Commission. IAEA is the International Atomic Energy Agency. The inspectors left Iraq during President Clinton's administration in 1998 when the U.S. government informed them that Iraq was about to be bombed.

According to the Senate Report, the intelligence community reached five main conclusions regarding Iraq and nuclear weapons as of December 2000. I set them forth in Exhibit 9:

Ex. 9
December 2000 ICA on Iraq's Nuclear Capability

The IAEA and UNSCOM had destroyed or neutralized Iraq's nuclear infrastructure, but it retained the foundation for future nuclear reconstitution.

Iraq was continuing low-level clandestine theoretical research & training and was attempting to buy dual-use items to reconstitute its nuclear program.

If Iraq acquired a significant quantity of fissile material through foreign assistance, it could have a crude nuclear weapon in a year.

It would take five to seven years for Iraq—with foreign assistance—to produce enough weapons-grade fissile material for a nuclear weapon.

Iraq did not appear to have reconstituted its nuclear weapons program.

Q. What would be the short version of the IC assessment on Iraq's nuclear capability at the time the President ordered the war plan?

A. Iraq had no nuclear weapons and no nuclear-weapons programs.

Q. Now, to answer the juror's question, Agent Crain, do we know exactly what Dearlove meant when he said intelligence was "being fixed around the policy" of invading Iraq?

A. No, not exactly. At a minimum, though, we know he meant that President Bush decided to invade Iraq first and looked for intelligence to justify his decision later.

Q. Do we have to rely on Dearlove's opinion to know that the President decided to invade Iraq without the benefit of intelligence?

A. No. The President made plans for and essentially started a war against Iraq without proof that Iraq was linked to 9/11 or that it was a nuclear threat. As a matter of fact, the President initiated all of this activity before he had even received a detailed intelligence briefing from the IC about Iraq. It is undisputed that the first time the President received such a briefing was in late December 2002.

When you consider intent to defraud, by the way, remember that this war planning and even the military escalation, occurred without notice to or authorization by Congress—and well outside of public view.

Q. Did the President request an updated NIE assessment on Iraq at any time before the invasion?

A. No. A new NIE on Iraq was, in fact, published in early October 2002, but only because Congress had demanded one in September. There is a fellow named Paul Pillar who was the CIA's National Intelligence Officer—the NIO—for Near East and Southeast Asia in 2001 when the Iraq war plan was ordered. As NIO, he coordinated all agency intelligence on Iraq, not just the CIA's. When he was asked in June of 2006 on PBS' *Frontline* whether any Executive Branch officials had asked him for intelligence about Iraq before the war, he said he did not receive any "requests from a policy-maker on Iraq until about a year into the war." Pillar did say, however, that some of his intelligence-council colleagues received requests that related to military planning.

In other words, while the President was insisting that he was deliberating about how to respond to Iraq, neither he nor any of his top officials bothered to formally request any information from our intelligence agencies, other than what they needed for military planning.

GRAND JUROR: I read that alternative intelligence shops were set up by Donald Rumsfeld and Douglas Feith at the Department of Defense. Is that true?

Q. Before we answer that directly, let me ask Agent Crain, does the term "fixing intelligence around the policy" have another meaning as well?

A. Yes, it can mean affirmatively trying to influence or change the intelligence-analysis product—the final conclusions that the analysts include in their assessments. It's also called "cooking intelligence" or "politicizing intelligence."

Q. Now the Senate Report and another report by the presidentially appointed Robb-Silberman Commission found that analysts weren't pressured in their analyses. Is there evidence that suggests those conclusions are wrong?

A. Yes. It is undisputed that Vice President Cheney and his close aide I. Lewis "Scooter" Libby made an unprecedented ten-plus visits to CIA headquarters in 2002 to question CIA agents. Defense Secretary Donald Rumsfeld relentlessly badgered his CIA briefer, and Deputy

National Security Adviser Stephen Hadley repeatedly pressed CIA Director George Tenet and his subordinates to rewrite analyses to present a stronger case against Iraq.

With all of this high-level attention, as Pillar explained on *Frontline*, politicization of intelligence on Iraq was inevitable. As of early 2002, he said, the administration's determination to invade Iraq was quite clear to people in the IC and "the questions every morning; the tasks; the requests to look into this angle one more time, turn over that rock again. If you didn't find anything last week, look again to see if there's something there [about connections between Iraq and 9/11]" would definitely skew analysts' work product.

Q. As our juror commented, the defendants did set up their own intelligence shops, didn't they? This is point four on Exhibit 1—beginning in October 2001, the defendants enlisted biased political appointees to find evidence to justify a war against Iraq.

A. Yes. Not long after President Bush and his senior advisers were informed that Iraq and Saddam Hussein had nothing to do with the 9/11 attacks and no working relationship with al Qaeda, Defense Secretary Rumsfeld had his subordinate Douglas Feith enlist Michael Maloof, a former aide to Richard Perle, and David Wurmser, a longtime advocate of forcible regime change, to "reevaluate" raw intelligence that had been discarded as unreliable in an effort to find evidence of the missing links between Iraq and al Qaeda.

Maloof was told Rumsfeld had requested the project because he was "not pleased" with the information he was getting from the IC. Maloof and Wurmser reported directly to Stephen Cambone—another regime-change advocate—who was Rumsfeld's key aide.

Then there was the OSP, the Office of Special Plans, which was a group of political appointees set up right in the Pentagon, by and under Feith. This group presented information directly to Rumsfeld, the National Security Adviser's Office, and the Office of the Vice President in August and September of 2002. Yet when Rumsfeld was asked about OSP in October 2002, he pretended that he could barely remember what it was. The American public knew nothing about this office until much later, and neither did CIA Director Tenet for at least part of its existence.

Q. Was Paul Pillar also familiar with OSP?

A. He said he was vaguely aware of it but did not consider it an intelligence unit—even though the administration was getting its key information from OSP, not the intelligence community. Instead, Pillar said, he considered OSP "more appropriately as extensions of a speechwriting staff since the mission was to come up with material for a public case."

Q. Agent Crain, it is necessary for the grand jury to decide whether the administration "cooked" intelligence in order to vote on the indictment in this case?

A. No.

Q. Why not?

A. Because an even bigger component of the fraud is how the administration served the intelligence—how they made their public case for war.

Q. That leads to the next items on Exhibit 1, correct?

A. Yes, items five and six, which cover the defendants' massive and fraudulent PR campaign to manipulate public opinion and push Congress into passing a resolution authorizing the use of force. If you will excuse my switching metaphors, it was a Cecil B. DeMille production. Agent Campbell, our resident English major, has titled it *Road to Resolution*.

Q. This is a good time for a break. See you all in fifteen minutes.

•••

10:30 P.M.

ASSISTANT U.S. ATTORNEY: Agent Crain, when did the defendants start setting up the stage for their *Road to Resolution* production?

A. They started as early as late September 2001, when they began describing Afghanistan as "Phase One" and the "beginning of the war on terror." Then, increasingly, they began telling the public that the United States had many enemies; that these "evil ones" were seeking WMD and harboring terrorists; and that we would not be secure as a nation until all of these as yet unnamed enemies or threats were defeated.

It was the boiling-frog technique, escalating the fear factor steadily and hoping that people wouldn't consciously notice what was happening.

Q. What is the boiling-frog technique?

A. A common technique of fraud and propaganda. If you drop a frog in boiling water, it will jump out, but if you drop it into cold water and slowly turn up the heat, it becomes desensitized and will boil to death without making any attempt to leave the premises. That's what the administration did. They desensitized the American public about Iraq by slowly ratcheting up the rhetorical heat. Before we knew it, we were cooked—I switched to a new metaphor again, didn't I?

Q. The President turned up the heat regarding Iraq even more in 2002, did he not?

A. Yes. In his January 29 State of the Union speech, the President asserted four facts about Iraq and all of them were deliberately deceptive.

Here's the first:

> Iraq continues to flaunt its hostility toward America and to support terror.

That was misleading. Some intelligence indicated that Saddam supported Palestinian terrorists, but the IC had no information that Saddam provided meaningful support to terrorists who threatened America. There was a small terrorist group called Al-Ansar in northern Iraq, but as White House officials all knew, it was neither under Saddam's control nor a threat to the United States. As the President and Vice President knew, the IC consistently said that Saddam had no cooperative relationship with al Qaeda.

The second one was:

> The Iraqi regime has plotted to develop anthrax, and nerve gas, and nuclear weapons for over a decade.

This falsely implied that Iraq currently had anthrax and nerve gas when we didn't know whether it did or not. The statement was also misleading because there was zero evidence that Iraq had either the capability or the intent to attack the United States with these substances.

Even worse, the President was implying that Iraq had nuclear weapons when Iraq had *never* had nuclear weapons, as the President well knew. In fact, the IC's unanimous opinion, included in a more recent assessment from December 15, 2001, was that Iraq had no nuclear-weapons programs and was not reconstituting them. Any nuclear equipment or materials in Iraq had been destroyed years ago. Even if the President, for some reason, subjectively believed his own assertion, he had no reasonable basis for saying it.

The third assertion was true, but nevertheless deceptive:

> This is a regime that has already used poison gas to murder thousands of its own citizens—leaving the bodies of mothers huddled over their dead children.

This is true, but as horrible as Saddam Hussein was, the administration never argued that we should remove him for humanitarian reasons, so it was a gratuitous fact included only to shock the American public and frighten them into thinking that Saddam Hussein would use the same tactics against people in the United States.

Q. Regarding the President's intent to deceive, is it significant that the poison-gas statement is detailed and the statements about terror and WMD are vague?

A. Yes. You've heard testimony that the President is actively involved in editing his speeches. You also know that he was trying to present the strongest possible case against Saddam Hussein. The President used graphic detail in making the one statement he could make that was fact-based but used only vague and ominous innuendo for the others. Why? Because he had no facts. Common sense tells you he was sidling right up to the line of outright falsehood, but did not want to step over it.

His statements were literally true but deliberately fraudulent.

Q. Is the President's fourth assertion even literally true?

A. No. He said:

> This is a regime that agreed to international inspections—then kicked out the inspectors. This is a regime that has something to hide from the civilized world.

As I mentioned before, the truth was that the UN inspectors left in 1998 because the U.S. government informed them that Iraq was about to be bombed. Bush and his aides were fully aware of that incident, but they nevertheless deceived the public about it repeatedly in the run-up to the invasion.

Q. In the State of the Union speech, President Bush used these four false premises to make an argument. What was the argument?

A. Precisely the one that Dearlove said the United States was going to use to justify the war: that Iraq posed a serious danger because of the "conjunction of terrorism and WMD."

Let me read you what the President argued in his January 2002 speech. Referring to Iran, North Korea, and Iraq, he said:

> States like these, and their terrorist allies, constitute an axis of evil, arming to threaten the peace of the world. By seeking weapons of mass destruction, these regimes pose a grave and growing danger. They could provide these arms to terrorists, giving them the means to match their hatred. They could attack our allies or attempt to blackmail the United States. In any of these cases, the price of indifference would be catastrophic.

Q. How does the President's argument relate to Dearlove's comment?

A. Like this: beyond establishing that Saddam was evil, the President's argument rested on three premises. The first was that Saddam had WMD. The second was that Saddam was connected to terrorists who hated the United States. The third was that he might provide the WMD he had to the terrorists.

In other words, the President was using the conjunction of weapons of mass destruction and terrorism to argue that Saddam posed a significant danger to the United States. It was the same argument, in fact, that the President had used in his May 2001 speech regarding Saddam Hussein. The President began using the conjunction of WMD and terrorism to frighten the American people about Saddam Hussein even before 9/11, but there were no facts to support the argument—ever.

Q. The argument wasn't going over well with the public in the first half of 2002, though, was it?

A. No, because it was a three-legged stool without a single solid leg.

GRAND JUROR: He's metaphor-switching.

A. I am. I apologize. Just to elaborate a bit: as I've already testified, the President knew he had no reasonable basis for asserting that Saddam had nuclear weapons or a connection to al Qaeda. He also knew that the third leg of the argument was wobbly, because the IC had consistently and unanimously reported that it was highly unlikely that Saddam would turn over WMD, if he even had any WMD, to terrorists. Mainly because Saddam didn't trust anyone. He didn't even trust his own generals, much less Islamic fundamentalists who hated his regime.

The bottom line is that not a single premise of the administration's argument was supported by facts, and its top officials knew it, which probably explains why they always argued their case is such ambiguous terms.

Nevertheless, it was their story and they were sticking to it.

Q. How did Iraq end up as a member of the "axis of evil"?

A. One of Bush's speechwriters, David Frum, was informed that the President wanted him to include language about Iraq in the 2002 State of the Union address. Frum took it from there. There was no deliberation about it.

Q. We're going to move on to another actor in the company: Vice President Richard, aka "Dick," Cheney.

Special Agent Crain, John Adams once said, "Facts are stubborn things." Was that a problem for the Bush-Cheney administration as they set the stage for war against Iraq?

A. Very much so. As early as fall 2001, reporters were beginning to ask about the administration's reference to Afghanistan as Phase One and its repeated juxtaposition of the "lessons of September 11" and Iraq. That was when Dick Cheney strolled onto the public stage. Actually onto *Meet the Press.*

On Sunday, December 9, host Tim Russert asked Cheney whether he had any evidence that connected Saddam Hussein to 9/11. Cheney replied that he did, that it was "pretty well confirmed" that the lead hijacker, Mohamed Atta, had met with the head of Iraqi intelligence in Prague in April of 2001.

Q. Did the Vice President have a reasonable basis for that representation?

A. No. The story was glaringly unreliable on its face. Based on the 9/11 Commission Report, among other sources, we now know that it was a thirdhand report from a Czech Republic intelligence service of a single, uncorroborated eyewitness observation from someone who had only come forward after seeing Atta's photograph in the newspaper post-9/11. The witness said he had seen Atta six months before, in April 2001, meeting with the head of Iraqi intelligence in Prague, but he was only 70 percent sure of the identification.

Q. Had the story been "confirmed" on December 9?

A. No, not in any valid way; it hadn't even been investigated yet.

The story had been publicly denied by the Czech government in mid-October and then inexplicably "confirmed" by them a week later. However, given the inherently weak nature of the story itself, Cheney could not rely in good faith on that "confirmation," especially when it followed so closely on the heels of a previous rejection of the report.

We now know, too, that the Czechs had not even investigated the story by December 2001. So I can't really fathom what they were purporting to "confirm." When the Czechs did investigate, they found records showing that the alleged Iraqi intelligence guy was not even in Prague at the time of the alleged meeting.

And remember, it was up to Cheney to affirmatively ask, *Where's the proof?* If he did not, he was making an assertion with reckless indifference to the truth. If he did ask, he would have known the Czechs had not yet investigated the case.

Most important, both the FBI and the CIA found the story unreliable almost from the beginning, but the FBI investigation was still going on. When it did end in March 2002, the FBI reported that there was no evidentiary support for the story. On the contrary, the evidence the FBI did find—cell phone and other records—showed that Atta was in Florida during the week in question. The FBI could not prove Atta's presence in Florida on the day of the meeting, but according to FBI Director Robert Mueller, "We ran down literally hundreds of thousands of leads and checked every record we could get our hands on, from flight reservations to car rentals to bank account" but found no evidence that showed Atta left the country during April 2001.

GRAND JUROR: We were wondering if we could break for lunch. We're stahvin'.

Q. I'm sorry. It *is* late. Let's meet back at 1:30.

•••

1:30 P.M.

ASSISTANT U.S. ATTORNEY: Back to the Mohamed Atta story, was there another technique that Bush administration officials used to mislead people about the basis they had for that story?

A. Yes. On February 23, 2002, Deputy Defense Secretary Wolfowitz was asked by a *San Francisco Chronicle* reporter whether he had any "convincing evidence to link Iraq to al Qaeda or its international network."

Wolfowitz said, "A lot of this stuff is classified and I really can't get into discussing it. . . . We also know that there are things that haven't been explained . . . like the meeting of Mohamed Atta with Iraqi officials in Prague. It just comes back to the fact that—"

At which point the reporter interrupted him, and asked, "Which is now alleged, right? There is some doubt to that?"

Then Wolfowitz replied, "Now this gets into classified areas again . . . I think the point, which I do think is fundamental, is that, the premise of your question seems to be, we wait for proof beyond a reasonable doubt. I think the premise of a policy has to be, we can't afford to wait for proof beyond a reasonable doubt."

Rumsfeld often used the same technique, implying that there was additional information that he could not reveal and then aggressively deflecting questions by suggesting that those who wanted actual evidence were being overly cautious.

Q. Just a few weeks later, behind the scenes, did Wolfowitz reveal his true thoughts about the Mohamed Atta story?

A. Yes, he told British Ambassador Meyer on March 17 that he thought the story was weak, and he even asked Meyer if *he* had any proof of it.

As an aside, the Downing Street Memos show that the British were trying to discourage the Americans from claiming any connection between Iraq and al Qaeda, because they thought it was an unsupportable argument that weakened the entire case. Wolfowitz did continue to assert to Meyer that there must be a link between Saddam Hussein and al Qaeda, however.

Q. Did Vice President Cheney stop using the Mohamed Atta story after the FBI report was issued?

A. No. He was still talking about it publicly as late as June 2004.

Q. How did he explain his thinking?

A. He would say, well, no one can prove it was *not* true.

Q. Is that, under the circumstances, also misleading?

A. Yes, because a government official trying to influence public decisions about a war is obligated to make sure that what he says is true before he says it. If something is only *possibly* true, and in this case extremely unlikely to be true, it is more than irresponsible for the Vice President of the United States to cite it as a basis for an invasion.

Q. Wolfowitz later made an interesting admission about the Iraq–al Qaeda issue, didn't he?

A. Yes, in the summer of 2003, conservative radio host Laura Ingraham asked him, "And when did you start to think that perhaps Iraq had something to do with [9/11]?"

Q. What did Wolfowitz say?

A. He said, "I'm not sure even now that I would say Iraq had something to do with [9/11]."

Q. Special Agent Crain, let's fast-forward to September 2002. Would it be accurate to say that on September 3, the White House was in dress rehearsal for the opening of the *Road to Resolution* production?

A. No. I think a better description would be that the troupe was squabbling behind the curtain, and they sent the

President's Press Secretary, Ari Fleischer, out on stage to keep the audience quiet. I would not have wanted to be in his shoes that day.

Q. Why not?

A. The September 3, 2002, White House briefing was the first since the President's return from his vacation, and the reporters had lots of questions about Iraq, to put it mildly.

August had been unusually chaotic for the Bush-Cheney administration because their famously on-message, unified public façade had cracked around the issue of Iraq, while Bush was out fishing at his ranch. The Vice President and Defense Secretary Rumsfeld did not want to "wrongfoot" Iraq by trying to get a new United Nations resolution passed and then hoping that Saddam would violate it, nor did they care much about international coalition building.

Secretary of State Powell, on the other hand, did want to go through the United Nations process. Also, according to Bob Woodward's book, *Plan of Attack*, Powell privately tried in early August to dissuade the President from proceeding with the war. The attempt failed, obviously, and Powell, for whatever reason, actively went along with the program after that as you will soon hear, which is why he is included in the proposed indictment.

Q. By that time, there was a public debate going on as well, wasn't there?

A. Yes, in August 2002, many noted foreign-policy experts—including President Bush, Sr.'s former National Security Adviser, Brent Scowcroft, and retiring House Majority Leader Republican Richard Armey—wrote articles arguing that an invasion of Iraq was not only strategically unwise but unjustified.

Opinion polls taken in mid-August also showed that support for an invasion was lukewarm. Only a slight majority of Americans supported it, and more than 50 percent did not think the President had made a sufficient case.

Q. I imagine the Vice President was not pleased with this situation?

A. No, he was not. Cheney took to the stage even before the show was to open—practically breathing fire—in successive speeches to VFW gatherings in late August. On August 26, in Tennessee, for example, he said, "Simply stated there is no doubt that Saddam Hussein now has weapons of mass destruction. There is no doubt that he is amassing them to use against our friends, against our allies, and against us."

Cheney then went on to denigrate the value of any UN inspections. He said:

> A person would be right to question any suggestion that we should just get inspectors back into Iraq, and then our worries will be over. Saddam has perfected the game of cheat and retreat, and is very skilled in the art of denial and deception. A return of inspectors would provide no assurance whatsoever of his compliance with UN resolutions. On the contrary, there is a great danger that it would provide false comfort that Saddam was somehow "back in his box."

Q. But one of the specific stories the Vice President cited to disparage inspections was not true, was it?

A. No. He said that in the spring of 1995, the inspectors had been close to declaring that Saddam Hussein's chemical-weapons programs had been shut down, when Hussein's son-in-law defected. The inspectors were led to a chicken farm, where they found evidence of a chemical-weapons program. What Cheney omitted to say, however, was that Hussein's son-in-law had not only said that all of the WMD had been destroyed, but he had also said the weapons inspections had been very effective.

Q. What was Colin Powell's response to Cheney's remarks?

A. Privately, I can only imagine, but Cheney's negative comments about inspections were the last thing Powell wanted to hear. He was in England at the time, trying to assure his counterpart, Foreign Secretary Jack Straw, that we would join the British in going to the United Nations—even if our mutual behind-the-scenes intent was to "wrongfoot" Saddam. Powell taped an interview with the BBC in which he assured the British audience of the United States' intent to seek a return of inspectors to Iraq, which was important for Blair on the domestic front.

Q. When did the interview air?

A. On September 1, so when Fleischer stepped up to the podium on September 3, the press was loaded for bear. They barraged Fleischer with questions, but he had his talking points down pat. Over and over again, he said that this is "much ado about no difference." He even maintained that Powell's and Cheney's statements reflected the exact same position.

It was an impressive, if slightly bizarre, performance. Fortunately, however, Fleischer only had to hold the press off for that one day, because the massive fraud campaign to convince the public and Congress to support the President's plan for an invasion of Iraq was set to premiere on the fourth of September. Everyone's lines had been written, and the appearances had been scheduled.

Q. Who had written the lines?

A. Mainly the White House Iraq Group.

Q. Let's go get some of that outstanding coffee downstairs.

•••

3:15 P.M.

ASSISTANT U.S. ATTORNEY: Everyone sufficiently recaffeinated? Over the break, I spoke with your foreperson about scheduling. She tells me that, given the choice between coming back for an extra day or having a slightly longer day tomorrow, you'd rather have the longer day. So we'll start at 8:30 tomorrow, having a shorter lunch, about forty-five minutes, and then try to finish up by 5:30 P.M. You should probably bring your lunches, unless you want to eat Turkey Surprise from downstairs.

Q. Agent Crain, in terms of criminal fraud techniques, how would you describe the defendants' pre–September 2002 conduct?

A. If the jurors look at the indictment, they will see that

allegations 61(a) through 61(d) all relate to the defendants' decision to invade Iraq; their true intent to invade; the extent of military buildup and force; the reason why they wanted Congress to pass a resolution authorizing military force; and the reason they wanted to go through the United Nations process of getting a resolution requiring Iraq to readmit weapons inspectors.

The technique of fraud the President and his advisers used as to those issues was mainly concealing material facts that they were obligated to disclose to the public and to Congress in order to make their representations regarding Iraq truthful.

It was very similar to the fraud charged in the Enron case, except, of course, much worse. For example, when Ken Lay said he had bought $4 million in stock but didn't tell them he had sold $24 million? The prosecutor's cross-examination highlighted the deceit perfectly: "When you told the employees that you're a buyer of stock, those employees, I think it's fair to say, would have liked to have known that you, in fact, were selling much more than you were buying."

I think it's fair to say that when the President and his aides were claiming that "no decision had been made" about Iraq, the public and Congress would have "liked to have known" that Bush had, in fact, not only finalized military plans but had been executing them for months—that the President had, in effect, already started a war.

GRAND JUROR: Weren't the representations that Iraq was a "grave and gathering danger" and Saddam Hussein was "amassing weapons of mass destruction" to blackmail the

United States made without reasonable basis and with reckless disregard for the truth?

A. Yes, even while they were concealing their decision to invade Iraq and occasionally telling outright lies, such as "the President has no war plans on his desk," White House officials were beginning to set up false pretenses to deceive the public about the *reasons* to invade Iraq.

Although the defendants continued and intensified these false pretenses both before and after the war started—repeating terrifying, yet largely baseless, assertions about the threat Iraq and Saddam Hussein posed to the United States—the public wanted proof. So did Congress. Even Democratic Senator Joseph Lieberman, who favored invading Iraq, accused the President of "saber-rattling" without providing support for his argument.

During press briefings by Press Secretary Ari Fleischer and Defense Secretary Donald Rumsfeld in the first week of September, the question that would get the award for most-often asked was some variation of, *When are we going to hear some evidence*?

That was where the White House Iraq Group stepped in, providing the defendants with their lines, and the more detailed they made those lines, the more fraudulent they became. The defendants had already begun making specific misrepresentations to back up their false generalities—such as the Mohamed Atta story, the claim that Saddam Hussein had kicked out the inspectors, Cheney's claim that he "knew" Iraq had nuclear weapons, and the half-truth about Saddam's son-in-law and chemical weapons—but both the general and specific falsehoods increased exponentially after September 1.

The misrepresentations that most increased when WHIG lifted the curtain on its extravaganza were the defendants' claimed justifications for invading Iraq, which are alleged in paragraph 65(e) of the indictment:

- Connections between Saddam Hussein's regime and 9/11, al Qaeda, or any terrorists whose primary animus was directed towards the U.S.
- Hussein's intent to attack the United States in any way
- Hussein's possession of nuclear weapons and the status of any nuclear weapons programs
- The status of any chemical and biological weapons stocks and programs
- And the urgency of any threat posed to the United States by Saddam Hussein.

Q. Agent Crain, earlier today you described the White House officials' case for war as a Cecil B. DeMille production. Is DeMille an unindicted coconspirator in this case?

A. No, but if he were, he'd be hard to arrest, considering that he's been dead for fifty years. Cecil B. De Mille was a movie director and producer who made big budget movies with huge casts and elaborate sets—by 1950s standards, anyway. Like *The Ten Commandments* and *War of the Worlds*, for which he was the executive producer.

Q. Did the defendants' 2002 production have something in common with *War of the Worlds*?

A. Yes, it did. The 1953 production of *War of the Worlds* was a remake of Orson Welles's radio play—which was itself a revision of H. G. Wells's novel from years before. The play was about a Martian invasion that scared the pants off of everyone when it aired in 1938. The White House Iraq Group's spectacle did precisely the same thing.

Q. The White House Iraq Group is also called WHIG?

A. Yes, and it was a group of advisers who met weekly beginning in July 2002—in the White House Situation Room—to develop and implement a strategy to sell the President's plan to invade Iraq.

Q. Why don't you name the members, and then we'll review who they are.

A. Karl Rove and Karen Hughes were the cochairs, and the others were Andrew Card, Mary Matalin, James R. Wilkinson, Nicholas E. Calio, Condoleezza Rice, Stephen Hadley, and I. Lewis "Scooter" Libby.

Q. Everyone knows Rice, Hadley, and Libby. Who's Karl Rove?

A. Karl Rove is a thirty-year veteran Republican political strategist, extremely tight with Bush, and influential. He and Karen Hughes coordinated Bush's presidential campaigns and Texas gubernatorial races. Bush calls Rove "the architect" of his 2004 reelection. In 2002, Rove was Special Adviser to the President and Director of the Office of

Strategic Initiatives—or OSI—which the President created in January 2001.

Q. What does OSI do?

A. According to the White House website, OSI "plans, develops and coordinates a long-range strategy for achieving Presidential priorities. The office conducts research and assists in message development."

Q. What does that mean?

A. The key words are "message development." The President claims he doesn't read public opinion polls, but he doesn't have to, because Rove *does*. At OSI, Rove gets public-opinion poll analyses and data from Matthew Dowd, another loyal Bush adviser, who works at the RNC—the Republican National Committee. Dowd, in turn, gets information from pollsters who research how best to word the President's "message" so the public will support his policies.

Q. I'll ask more about that later, but, first, who is Karen Hughes?

A. Karen Hughes is also a political strategist, probably even more influential with Bush than Rove. She was appointed Counselor to the President in 2001 and, according to Laura Flanders's book, *Bushwomen*, Hughes "sat in on every meeting, oversaw the offices of press secretary, communications and speechwriting" and had each department's communications director report to her.

Q. Who are the others?

A. Mary Matalin has been a Republican political consultant for over twenty years, and James Wilkinson was a key Bush strategist for the 2000 election. Matalin had two job titles—Counselor to Vice President Cheney and Assistant to President Bush—and was almost as powerful as Rove and Hughes.

Andrew Card, of course, was the President's Chief of Staff, and Nicholas Calio was the President's congressional liaison.

In short, WHIG's members were from the White House's innermost circles, and their purpose was politics and PR. Their show premiered, as I testified previously, with the President's September 4 "open dialogue" remarks.

Q. On that day, the President said he was starting a dialogue with Congress, the American people, and who else?

A. Our "friends in the world." And to make it appear that he was doing just that, Bush opened the OGC—Office of Global Communications—in July of 2002, to "formulate and coordinate messages to foreign audiences" and "supervise America's image abroad."

Q. Supervising America's foreign image wasn't exactly a cakewalk, was it?

A. No. I should also mention that OGC and WHIG coordinated their huge public-relations effort with Alastair Campbell, Prime Minister Blair's Communications Director.

Q. Is there evidence of a connection between the President's push for an invasion of Iraq and the politics of the congressional election scheduled for November 2002?

A. Yes, there is. For starters, as I've described, most WHIG members were political strategists, not policy experts. Karen Hughes was actually on the *payroll* of the Republican National Committee when she worked with WHIG.

Also, Rove had been advising Republicans to use the "war on terror" as an election issue since January of 2002. Then, in June, to someone's great chagrin, I'm sure, a disk containing PowerPoint presentations designed for Republican campaign groups was found in Washington's Lafayette Park. The presentation had two parts, one specifically attributed to Ken Mehlman, the other to Karl Rove.

Q. Who is Ken Mehlman?

A. He's now the RNC Chairman, but in 2002 he directed the White House Office of Political Affairs.

In Mehlman's section—

Q. How do we know the disk is authentic?

A. Both Press Secretary Ari Fleischer and Mehlman acknowledged that it was.

Anyway, Mehlman's slides showed Republicans being vulnerable to losing twenty-five House of Representatives' seats in the November election, but the Democrats only possibly losing ten, the point being that the Republicans considered their position precarious. They wanted a majority in both houses of Congress, so the President's legislative efforts would have smooth sailing.

Rove's section included historical polling data that showed a correlation between a president's approval ratings and his party's success in midterm elections. His slides reiterated that Republicans should "focus on war" and mentioned that Bush would vigorously campaign for Republican candidates in the fall.

Q. Did the President do that?

A. He certainly did: five campaign appearances in the first week of September alone, as you can see from Exhibit 11a, *Act One: Road to Resolution*. At each one, he talked about Iraq.

Q. Before we turn to that, why did you and Agent Campbell come up with this title, *Road to Resolution*? Apart from that you both obviously need vacations.

A. Well, "Resolution" refers to the congressional resolution authorizing the use of military force that the defendants started pushing for in early September. Cecil B. DeMille came to mind because a critical component of the President's fraud was its sheer *scale*. It involved not only the highest Executive Branch officials and appointees, but also thousands of employees in the Executive Office of the President, the Vice President's Office, the National Security Adviser's Office, and the Departments of Defense and State.

That fact helps explain why the fraud was so effective. But it's also important because, even before you consider the substance of the defendants' many fraudulent statements, the size and complexity of the operation proves how *intentional* it was.

And, amazingly, Karl Rove and Andrew Card pretty much admitted the entire scheme on September 6, 2002.

The article about their statements comes darned close to being a smoking-gun document.

Q. What article is that?

A. From the *New York Times.* The beginning is excerpted in Exhibit 10:

Ex. 10
September 7, 2002
TRACES OF TERROR: THE STRATEGY
Bush Aides Set Strategy to Sell Policy on Iraq
By Elisabeth Bumiller

> WASHINGTON, Sept. 6—White House officials said today that the administration was following a meticulously planned strategy to persuade the public, the Congress and the allies of the need to confront the threat from Saddam Hussein. . . .

Q. Is it clear that information in the article was leaked by Bush-Cheney administration officials?

A. Yes.

Q. Why do you say that?

A. Mainly because Karl Rove and Andrew Card are quoted by name in it. Card is quoted as saying, "From a marketing point of view, you don't introduce new products in August." The article also mentions that the administration had just begun a "full-scale lobbying campaign" on Capitol Hill, which Rove described as "a necessary step." No White House official ever disavowed anything in the article, which they would have done if they disputed it.

Q. Obviously from this excerpt we can glean that the events that followed—the defendants' statements and responses to various events—were deliberate, correct?

A. Yes. The article also says that the President, Hughes, Card, and Rove had begun planning the strategy in July, and "a centerpiece" of it was to use Bush's upcoming speech commemorating the 9/11 attacks to "help move Americans toward support of action against Iraq, which could come early next year."

Q. In other words, they intended to tie the marketing of the war against Iraq to 9/11, even though they knew the two were unconnected?

A. Yes.

Q. What else does the article reveal about the defendants' intent?

A. It says, "the White House wants a resolution approving the use of force in Iraq to be approved in the next four to five weeks." So, despite Bush's earlier promise of "open dialogue," his aides were admitting that they had already decided what they wanted to do about Iraq—and when they wanted to do it.

It was also clear that Bush and his advisers intended to do whatever they had to do to ram their plan through. The article notes that congressional leaders were skeptical about whether Iraq posed an "imminent threat," but White House officials told the *Times* they would reveal "higher levels of intelligence" to make their case and, according to an unnamed official, "In the end it will be difficult for someone to vote against it." In other words, the Bush-Cheney administration's deliberate strategy was not just to persuade Congress directly, but to pressure Congress by manipulating the opinions of their constituents.

Q. Which is why the entire fraudulent production, and not simply defendants' direct statements to Congress, would be considered an effort to interfere with and obstruct Congress's lawful functions of overseeing foreign affairs and authorizing the expenditure of government funds?

A. That is exactly right.

GRAND JUROR: One point? So it was just as that British Defense Secretary Hoon said at the Downing Street meeting—I wrote it down: "The most likely timing in US minds for military action to begin was January, with the timeline beginning 30 days before the US Congressional elections"?

A. That's right—just as Hoon said.

Q. Time to call it a day. We'll meet back here tomorrow at 8:30 A.M.

•••

END OF DAY SIX

UNITED STATES v. GEORGE W. BUSH et al.
GRAND JURY PRESENTATION

Testimony of FBI Special Agent Daniel Crain

8:30 A.M.

ASSISTANT UNITED STATES ATTORNEY: Good morning, and thank you for getting here early. Could someone see where Agent Crain is? [Whereupon the witness enters the room and is sworn]

Q. When we left off yesterday, we were talking about the defendants'—and White House Iraq Group's—"meticulously planned" strategy to obtain a resolution authorizing force before Congress adjourned for the election season. That was already being implemented by September 7, when the article we were talking about yesterday came out, wasn't it?

A. Yes, it was.

Q. How do you know?

A. From numerous sources, including the White House website, which chronicles the President's appearances and publishes the texts of most of his speeches. It also contains press-briefing transcripts and news releases that cover everything from significant public events to Leif Erikson Day—which is October 9, by the way. I've read everything on the website from September 2001 through September 2004, along with items from outside that period.

I have no life.

Q. And Exhibits 11a through 11f summarize the Iraq-related postings on the White House website from September 1 through October 16, 2002, correct?

A. Yes, except for the Press Secretary's briefings.

Q. Why that time frame?

A. *Road to Resolution* opened in early September and closed on October 16, when the President announced that Congress had passed the authorization he wanted.

Q. Let's look at Exhibit 11a:

Ex. 11a
Act One: *Road to Resolution*

SEPTEMBER

2 President Thanks Workers at Labor Day Picnic [2002 campaign, Pennsylvania]

3 Statement by Press Secretary [re: meeting planned with Prime Minister of Canada]

4 President Discusses Foreign Policy with congressional Leaders [White House]

5 President Focuses on Economy and War on Terrorism in Kentucky Speech [2002 campaign, Louisville, Kentucky]

Remarks by the President at Chris Chocola for Congress, and Indiana Victory 2002 Finance Dinner [2002 campaign, Indiana]

Remarks by the President at Anne Northup for Congress Luncheon [2002 cam-

paign, Louisville, Kentucky]
Remarks by the President at South Bend, Indiana Welcome [2002 campaign, South Bend, Indiana]

6 Statement by Press Secretary [re: meeting planned with Prime Minister of Portugal]

7 President Bush, Prime Minister Blair Discuss Keeping the Peace [Crawford, Texas]

Q. Jurors, you recall—I hope—Agent Crain's testimony that the scale and complexity of the White House production showed the deliberation that informed their fraud. We'll be using Exhibits 11a through f to explain that point and to highlight some significant events along the road to resolution. Agent Crain, could you explain Exhibit 11a?

A. Sure. The numbers on the left are dates, and the unbracketed text is reproduced verbatim from the White House website. Most entries reflect Bush's speeches or appearances, and I've indicated in brackets the place where he was speaking. So, for example, the text for the September 2, 2002 entry, "President Thanks Workers at Labor Day Picnic," comes from the White House website. The President made the speech in Pittsburgh, Pennsylvania.

Q. Why is a Labor Day speech on this chart?

A. Because the President began hinting at a link between Saddam Hussein and 9/11 in that appearance. He said, "We got hit on September 11th and we know there's an enemy out there that hates freedom." He then added, "We love freedom" and assured his audience that he considered protection of the "homeland" his biggest job.

GRAND JUROR: Why do some entries indicate "2002 campaign"?

A. From reading the transcripts of the President's speeches, including references to Republican candidates who attended the events, I've determined that many of Bush's fall 2002 appearances were either solely or partly campaign stops, even if the White House website didn't say so. The September 5 speech, entitled, "President Focuses on Economy and War on Terrorism in Kentucky Speech," was actually a campaign pitch for Republican candidate Anne Northup.

GRAND JUROR: Was the "South Bend, Indiana Welcome" actually a campaign stop, then?

A. Yes, the White House website frequently uses the term "Welcome" as a euphemism for a campaign speech.

Q. You've talked about recurring themes that White House officials stressed during this period, such as that the President had made no decision about Iraq and that he was consulting with Congress, the public, and our allies. Did these themes correspond to the findings of public-opinion polls?

A. Yes, without going into detail, in the run-up to the war, polls consistently showed that Americans would be more favorably disposed toward invading Iraq if the Bush-Cheney administration obtained the support of Congress and of our allies beforehand. Which, I believe, explains the almost absurd repetition of this theme of consultation by the

President and his aides, especially in September, and their pointed effort to demonstrate that they were cooperating.

The entries labeled "Statement by the Press Secretary," on Exhibit 11a, for example, are announcements of planned meetings with foreign leaders. The President, Ari Fleischer, and other administration officials mentioned such "consultations" repeatedly before the war.

Q. What other themes emerged in the first week of WHIG's production?

A. The themes evolved somewhat in response to events and criticisms, but a key one that week was that Saddam Hussein was a horrible person who had "poisoned his own people," had invaded other countries before, and was a murderous dictator. These representations were true, of course, but Bush used them to deceive the public by suggesting that Saddam Hussein wanted to attack us, definitely had WMD, and would be willing to supply them to terrorists—none of which was true. Here is what the President said in Kentucky on September 5, 2002: We can't let the "world's worst leaders blackmail, threaten, and hold freedom-loving nations hostage with the world's worst weapons."

GRAND JUROR: Isn't that what he said in May of 2001 also?

A. Yes, the President's story has never changed. Closely linked to this argument was another theme: urgency. Here is Bush on September 5 again: "We must deal with threats to our security today, before it can [*sic*] be too late." Although the President would later claim he never said the threat was urgent, his own White House website shows that he and his aides conveyed precisely that message repeatedly before the war.

Here, for example, is Press Secretary Ari Fleischer on September 4, 2002, explaining why the administration had suddenly decided that sanctions were ineffective, though they had successfully contained Iraq prior to 9/11:

> As the President said, America's worst nightmare is that Saddam Hussein will link up with terrorists like al Qaeda, who have already demonstrated a willingness to attack the United States. And were Saddam Hussein able to transfer any of the WMD—the chemical, biological weapons, or nuclear weapons that he seeks—to these organizations, it would be too late for the United States to do anything.

On the same day, the President said, "Doing nothing in the face of a grave threat to the world is not an option." And here is what he said on October 2, 2002: "The Iraqi regime is a threat of unique urgency . . . it has developed weapons of mass destruction." Both of those assertions were false and fraudulent, because as Director Tenet testified in February 2004, the intelligence community had never informed the President that Saddam Hussein presented an imminent or urgent threat.

Q. What was the topic of the September 7, 2002, event called "President Bush, Prime Minister Blair Discuss Keeping the Peace"?

A. War.

Q. Would you care to expand on that?

A. As part of his effort to convince the public that he was consulting with allies, the President made a big show of inviting British Prime Minister Tony Blair to his Crawford, Texas, ranch to talk about Iraq, even though privately they had been strategizing for months about "wrongfooting" Saddam Hussein by insisting on the return of inspectors.

In remarks to the press after their meeting, they made it clear that they were determined to invade Iraq, referring to Saddam Hussein as a "real threat" at least five times in fewer than ten minutes.

They really crossed the line though when they tried to "prove" Saddam Hussein's ongoing pursuit of nuclear weapons. They cited what they implied was a "recent" report that, as Blair described it, showed "what has been going on at [Iraq's] former nuclear weapons sites," by which he was suggesting that there was nuclear-related work then occurring in Iraq. Bush added, "I would remind you that when the inspectors first went into Iraq and were denied, finally denied, access, a report came out of the Atomic—the IAEA—that they were six months away from developing a weapon. I don't know what more evidence we need."

Both Blair and Bush deliberately misled the public by implying there was a recent report, because, as they well knew, the International Atomic Energy Agency inspectors had not been in Iraq since 1998.

Q. Did the IAEA's 1998 report even say that Iraq was six months away from developing a weapon?

A. No, far from it. The IAEA reported that it had found no evidence that Iraq had produced nuclear weapons, retained the physical capability to produce "weapons-usable nuclear material or having clandestinely obtained such material."

Q. Just to sum up, during Act One of WHIG's *Road to Resolution*, the President made seven public appearances—at the White House, in Crawford, and at campaign stops in Pennsylvania, Kentucky, and Indiana—where he warned the American public, without any reasonable basis whatsoever, about the dire threat that Iraq posed to the United States?

A. That is true.

Q. Other White House officials were making such public statements as well, weren't they?

A. Yes. Vice President Cheney had, of course, begun making such statements in August, but Defense Secretary Rumsfeld held a press briefing in the first week of September as did State Department spokesperson Richard Boucher and his Defense Department counterpart Victoria Clarke. They all repeated the same points, as did Ari Fleischer, who had a press briefing nearly every day.

But all of those appearances were previews. Sunday, September 8 was the big day.

Q. What happened on September 8, 2002?

A. Well, as I testified earlier, the *New York Times* had reported the day before that White House officials would be revealing "higher levels of intelligence" to make their case for war.

The defendants apparently decided to reveal this intelligence by leaking it to the *New York Times*. The September 8 Sunday *Times* had an article by reporter Judith Miller, dated September 7, 2002, and headlined, "U.S. Says Hussein Intensifies Quest for A-Bomb Parts." Among other things, the article quoted unnamed "Bush administration officials" as saying that Iraq had started a "worldwide hunt for materials to make an atomic bomb." The article also reported that, within the past fourteen months, Iraq had tried to buy thousands of specially designed aluminum tubes, which "American officials" believe were intended to be used as components of centrifuges to make enriched uranium.

Q. Did you investigate media reports to determine whether the Bush administration disavowed this article? Did they ever say they hadn't provided this information?

A. No to both questions. It was quite the opposite.

Q. What do you mean?

A. They embraced it. That same morning, five administration officials appeared on separate Sunday talk shows to argue that Saddam Hussein presented a grave threat to the United States. Three of those officials—Vice President Cheney, Condoleezza Rice, and Colin Powell—said that the Iraqis were trying to buy aluminum tubes that would be used for nuclear centrifuges. Rice claimed, specifically, that the tubes were "only really suited" for nuclear use and Powell and Cheney said essentially the same thing. Powell and Cheney attributed the story to the *New York Times* article from the morning.

Q. And you have excerpted those comments in Exhibit 12,

which we need to look at before we finish with Exhibits 11b through 11f?

A. Yes, the jurors should have it in their packets:

Ex. 12
September 8, 2002
Re: Aluminum Tubes

RICHARD B. CHENEY, VICE PRESIDENT (on NBC's *Meet the Press*):
"He [Saddam Hussein] is trying, through his illicit procurement network, to acquire the equipment he needs to be able to enrich uranium—specifically, aluminum tubes."

NATIONAL SECURITY ADVISER CONDOLEEZA RICE (on CNN's *Late Night with Wolf Blitzer*):
The tubes "are only really suited for nuclear weapons programs, centrifuge programs."

COLIN POWELL, SECRETARY OF STATE (on *Fox News*):
"And as we saw in reporting just this morning, he [Saddam] is still trying to acquire, for example, some of the specialized aluminum tubing one needs to develop centrifuges that would give you an enrichment capability."

GRAND JUROR: I was just thinking . . .

Q. That's good.

GRAND JUROR: Well, weren't Cheney and Powell attributing to the *New York Times* information that had been leaked by someone in their own administration?

A. It appears so. That is a common MO of Bush et al. They plant information with friendly reporters and then pretend to rely on it. It's like money laundering—hiding the source of funds through circuitous transactions—except the currency this President launders is information. Why government officials would want anyone to think they were using newspaper reports to formulate United States foreign policy is beyond me.

Q. Okay, it's ten o'clock. Let's take a fifteen-minute break, and we'll pick up with Agent Crain's testimony about those tubes.

•••

10:15 A.M.

ASSISTANT U.S. ATTORNEY: Before we bring in our witness, I want to explain a few additional legal points and review several that we've already covered.

Remember Agent Estrada's testimony about the obligations that apply to White House officials once they take their oaths of office? We may be increasingly accustomed to public officials deceiving us, but it is still the law of the United States that once politicians become Executive Branch officials, they are legally required to be honest and forthright about public matters. So when, as you'll hear more about today, White House officials affirmatively undertake to persuade the public to go along with their plans for war, they are obligated to ensure that the representations they make in the course of that campaign of persuasion are true.

That means the whole truth, not just the "good stuff" for their side. A government official is not legally entitled to tell the public that a certain fact is true merely because there is *some* support for it. As I mentioned before, politicians may be able to rely on "plausible deniability" as a defense, but criminal defendants cannot.

White House officials, just like CEOs, are legally required to make sure that they have a reasonable, factual basis for their assertions *before* they make them. They cannot recklessly make claims and then scramble to support them later with newly discovered evidence.

Moreover, if they have notice that an assertion they are making is not true, or even dubious, they are legally obligated to inquire further. The law does not allow government officials *or* corporate officials to avoid responsibility for their false statements by remaining willfully blind in the face of information that would cause a reasonable person to make inquiry.

Another legal principle you need to understand is that of good-faith reliance. Remember the testimony about former CIA analyst Paul Pillar's description of the incessant questioning of CIA agents by Executive Branch officials and his observations of the Office of Special Plans? Officials who know that the information they are receiving comes from biased sources or from intelligence analysts whom they had improperly tried to influence cannot legally claim to have relied in good faith on that information.

Finally, some of you may, after hearing all of the evidence in the case, decide that Congress or the public should have known they were being misled. And there was, of course, a significant minority of Americans who were not misled by the defendants' misrepresentations, but it is not a defense to criminal fraud that the victims should have known better, or that some weren't actually defrauded. Those are civil fraud considerations, but in criminal cases, the focus is on the *defendants*' efforts to intentionally deceive, not whether the victim should have been more savvy or suspicious.

With that, could one of you retrieve Agent Crain from the hallway? [Whereupon the witness enters the room and is sworn]

Q. Agent Crain, what were the most significant misrepresentations the defendants made regarding weapons of mass destruction?

A. The ones that supported their claim that Saddam Hussein had reconstituted his nuclear weapons program.

Q. What two specific claims did Bush and his aides make to buttress that general allegation?

A. To be clear, they sometimes even said they "knew" that Iraq had nuclear *weapons*—a claim which was, of course, devoid of factual support. But the specifics they offered as proof of Iraq's nuclear weapons *programs* were, first, that the Iraqis had tried to buy yellowcake—which can be used to make enriched uranium—from Africa, and, second, that they were trying to purchase certain aluminum tubes with the intent to use them in nuclear-related centrifuges.

Q. Jurors, we don't have time to look in depth at all of the defendants' fraudulent statements about WMD, but we're going to examine the aluminum-tubes statements in some detail to illustrate just how knowing and intentional their fraud was. What sources have you reviewed, Agent Crain, to compare the defendants' public representations about these tubes to the information that was available to them behind the scenes when they made the statements?

A. Mainly, I've analyzed the findings in the Report of the Senate Select Committee on Intelligence and in a similar report by the Robb-Silberman Commission, which was a presidentially appointed group that examined pre–Iraq War intelligence. I've also reviewed numerous media reports.

Q. First, what is a centrifuge?

A. A centrifuge is any machine—a clothes dryer, for example—that spins substances rapidly to separate out liquids or heavier gases from lighter gases. Certain specially designed centrifuges that spin at very, very high speeds can be used to separate out U-235, which is a heavy, unstable uranium that's used in nuclear-fission bombs.

Q. Did the intelligence community agree in September 2002 that the aluminum tubes the Iraqis had tried to buy were "only really suitable," as Condoleezza Rice put it, for use in nuclear centrifuges?

A. No, the intelligence community did not even agree that the tubes were *suitable* for nuclear centrifuges. There was a vigorous debate within the IC about the intended use of these tubes. I'll explain that in detail in a minute, but just so people have a sense of the issue, the CIA took the position that these tubes were probably suitable for use in nuclear centrifuges. That's the opinion the defendants seized on, but it did not represent a consensus. It was only half the story.

The agency that the President's own commission—the Robb-Silberman Commission—described as the "primary repository of expertise" on nuclear matters, which was the Department of Energy, had analyzed the tubes and the circumstances of their attempted procurement and had concluded that the tubes were decidedly *unsuitable* for nuclear centrifuges. The DOE concluded that the tubes were well suited for use in the manufacture of artillery rockets, and they believed that was the purpose for which the Iraqis were trying to buy them.

Q. Did any of the agencies ever say that the tubes were *only really suitable* for use in nuclear centrifuges?

A. No. Rice's statement was not backed up by *any* intelligence information whatsoever.

Q. This debate among the agencies that you referred to, when did it begin?

A. It began in the spring of 2001, when the CIA learned that Iraq was trying to order 6,000 custom-made aluminum tubes.

Q. The Iraqis' specifications are important to the debate, aren't they?

A. Yes. The tubes were to be cut to a length of 900 millimeters, which is about three feet long. The outer diameter was 81 millimeters, or about 4 inches, and the wall was 3.3 millimeters, the approximate thickness of two pennies set on top of each other.

The Iraqis also specified that the aluminum was to be anodized, which means covered with a protective coating.

Q. What did the CIA do after receiving this information?

A. They included it in the President's Daily Briefing—called a PDB—which is a highly classified report provided only to the president, vice president, and a few others. This PDB is still classified, but the Senate Report stated that the CIA described the tubes as "most likely intended" for a uranium-enrichment program.

Then, on April 10, 2001, the CIA issued a Senior Intelligence Executive Brief, which opined that these tubes had "little use other than for a uranium-enrichment program," although it noted that using *aluminum* tubes for a nuclear centrifuge would be "inefficient and a step backwards" for the Iraqis.

Q. What was the CIA referring to?

A. In the early 1990s, after the first Gulf War, inspectors discovered, and destroyed, prototype tubes that the Iraqis had made for use in a nuclear centrifuge. They were made from a material called carbon fiber that was better-suited to nuclear applications than aluminum.

Q. Did the Department of Energy, or DOE, nuclear-weapons experts weigh in?

A. Yes. The next day, the DOE published a Daily Intelligence Highlight which stated that the centrifuge application could not be ruled out but was unlikely.

Q. What reasons did DOE give?

A. Well, DOE provided more extensive analysis later, but its April 2001 report noted four reasons for its conclusion that the tubes were not intended for a nuclear program:

One: The specified diameter was too small for nuclear-centrifuge use;

Two: The design was quite different from those the Iraqis were known to have;

Three: The quantity of tubes the Iraqis were seeking—six thousand—indicated large-scale production that would require high-volume purchases of other parts—which was not occurring; and

Four: The manner of procurement—open negotiation with multiple vendors—was inconsistent with the operation of a secretive nuclear-weapons program.

The DOE believed the tubes were intended to be used in military rocket production but didn't know which type of rocket.

Q. By September 8, 2002, how many U.S. intelligence-agency analyses about these tubes had been issued?

A. Fourteen that I'm aware of.

Q. How many of those published assessments discussed problems with—or differences of opinion about—the CIA's contention that the Iraqis wanted the tubes for nuclear-centrifuge use?

A. Twelve.

Q. Were there also non-U.S. intelligence agency reports that mentioned the debate or contrary opinions about the tubes?

A. Yes. At least three: two from the IAEA that were cabled to the U.S. State Department in the summer of 2002 and a July 2002 report from Australia's Defense Intelligence Organization that acknowledged the U.S. agencies' debate about the tubes but described the nuclear end-use evidence as "patchy and inconclusive."

Q. Did the debate consist of CIA agents saying that "the tubes are for nuclear centrifuges" and DOE experts responding, as my little niece used to say, "Not!"?

A. Oh no. Although the CIA did not explain its opinion until August 2002, the DOE wrote fairly detailed explanations in April and May 2001, and then, on August 17, 2001, issued an eight-page report that set out its reasoning and explanations in detail. So the Bush-Cheney administration officials had extremely specific and comprehensive notice that the CIA's opinion was dubious.

Q. In other words, they had reason to inquire further about the truth and accuracy of the claims they were making about these tubes?

A. That would be an understatement, especially because the main source for the CIA's conclusion was a CIA agent with a mechanical engineering background, but the DOE experts were well-known and accomplished nuclear scientists with extensive experience.

The scientists who worked on the August 17 analysis included Dr. Jon A. Kreykes, who was head of Oak Ridge National Laboratory's national-security advanced technology group; Dr. Duane F. Starr, an expert on nuclear proliferation threats; Dr. Edward Von Halle, a retired Oak

Ridge nuclear expert; and Dr. Houston G. Wood III, a University of Virginia engineering professor who was a well-known consultant at Oak Ridge.

Q. What did they conclude?

A. The nuclear experts concluded that a nuclear-centrifuge use for the aluminum tubes was, quote, "credible but unlikely."

Q. What reasons did they give for that assessment?

A. The first was the one the CIA had mentioned in April: that aluminum was inferior to the carbon fiber the Iraqis had already tried before the first Gulf War and to another material the Iraqis had previously procured called maraging steel, which is used in golf clubs. As Dr. Wood put it, "Aluminum was a huge step backwards."

Q. The DOE experts believed the specified dimensions were not suitable either, correct?

A. Yes, the four-inch diameter was far smaller than that used in any known operational centrifuge.

Q. The fact that the diameter was far too small was one of several critical considerations that led DOE to conclude the tubes were not intended to be used in nuclear-weapons manufacture, wasn't it?

A. Yes, absolutely, because while the Iraqis might have been able to adjust other dimensions of the tubes, it was impossible to make the diameter larger.

The tubes the Iraqis specified were also too thick. They would have to be machined to one-third of their thickness, which was an extremely time-consuming process, because a nuclear centrifuge application required the tubes to be only about one millimeter, slightly less than the thickness of a dime.

The length the Iraqis ordered was too long for a possible nuclear-centrifuge application. Each tube would have to be cut to less than half the length the Iraqis had specified.

Another problem was that the Iraqis were requiring the surface of the tubes to be anodized, which means covered with a protective coating. The DOE scientists pointed out that this coating would have to be removed because the chemicals it was made of would react adversely to the uranium gases.

Finally, the tolerance—the level of precision to which the dimensions have to be cut—was two to five times looser than that needed for a nuclear-centrifuge application.

GRAND JUROR: In other words, to conclude that the Iraqis intended to use these tubes in a nuclear centrifuge, you'd have to assume that they deliberately ordered tubes that were made from inferior material, not cut as precisely as they needed, three times too thick, more than twice as long, half the diameter needed, and coated with something they'd have to take off?

A. Correct.

Q. Let's take our lunch break. We'll see you all at 1:15 P.M.

•••

1:15 P.M.

ASSISTANT U.S. ATTORNEY: Agent Crain, what did a DOE expert testify to the Senate Committee about the efficacy of using these tubes in a nuclear centrifuge?

A. He said, "You could also turn your new Yugo into a Cadillac" if you worked at it enough. The DOE expert also pointed out that, if Iraq really was trying to make centrifuges out of these tubes, "We should just give them the tubes."

Q. Because they would never get anywhere with that effort?

A. Right.

Q. On the other hand, the DOE found that the tubes were *well-suited* for use in multiple-rocket launchers, right?

A. Yes. The tubes were virtually identical to ones that the IAEA had found at Iraq's Nasser rocket facility in Baghdad in 1996, after Iraq declared them in the course of the weapons-inspection process. The Iraqis were trying to reverse-engineer an Italian rocket called the Medusa. The type of aluminum the Iraqis ordered for these tubes was, the DOE analysis reported, "the material of choice" for low-cost rocket systems.

Q. Did White House officials continue to mislead the public about the likely intended use of the tubes despite the fifteen intelligence-community reports that described the controversy and the four to five IC reports that explained why the nation's foremost nuclear experts believed the CIA's opinion was wrong?

A. Oh yeah. In his September 12, 2002, speech to the U.N., the President asserted that Iraq had a reconstituted nuclear weapons program and then stated, "Saddam Hussein has made several attempts to buy high-strength aluminum tubes used to enrich uranium for a nuclear weapon." The same day, WHIG posted a paper on the White House website called "A Decade of Deception and Defiance" that asserted:

> Iraq has stepped up its quest for nuclear weapons and has embarked on a worldwide hunt for materials to make an atomic bomb. In the last 14 months, Iraq has sought to buy thousands of specially designed aluminum tubes which officials believe were intended as components of centrifuges to enrich uranium.

Q. These statements are fraudulent in several respects, aren't they?

A. Yes. The general assertions, made both in the President's speech and the White House posting, that Iraq had renewed its efforts to acquire nuclear weapons approach the level of outright lies because they are entirely without basis.

The specific assertions, however, are more along the lines of the old Listerine ad technique: literally true, yet misleading. You can really appreciate the deliberation that went into the administration's deceit, though, by noting the differences between the President's UN address and the WHIG posting. Presumably, the more sophisticated UN audience knew that there was little, if any, proof that the Iraqis wanted these tubes for use in a nuclear centrifuge. So the President didn't say that to them; instead, he *implied* it by juxtaposing the aluminum-tubes reference to the claim that Iraq was trying to resume nuclear-weapons production and then describing the *tubes* as ones "used to enrich uranium for a nuclear weapon."

The audience for the web posting, however, would have been broader and less sophisticated. The White House Iraq Group posted such papers for many purposes, but one was to provide the media with prewritten "hard data" to include in its reports. In "A Decade of Deception and Defiance," WHIG stretched the truth even further than usual, asserting that "officials believe" the tubes were intended "as components of centrifuges used to enrich uranium."

Sure, *some officials* believed that, including some in the CIA who were trying to satisfy the President's obvious desire to have a justification for invading Iraq, but it was not the consensus opinion, and it was specifically contradicted by the government's own nuclear experts. So, in criminal-law terms, whether you describe the falsehood as literally true but misleading or as concealing material information, the bottom line is the same: it was fraudulent. Yet, the defendants and many other White House spokespersons repeated it over and over again.

Q. Not long after the September 8 roadshow and the President's speech to the United Nations, the existence of the internal intelligence community debate began to surface publicly, didn't it?

A. Yes. By virtue of the fifteen IC reports, the President and his advisers had more than ample notice, behind the scenes, to require them to question the validity of their claims *before* September 8, 2002. After the President's speech, however, they received even *more* information, both publicly and privately, that cast doubt on their aluminum-tubes allegations.

Q. Why don't you review some of that evidence quickly?

A. The first article that mentioned the difference of opinion within the intelligence community was a *New York Times* piece that appeared on September 13, 2002. The article reported that a "senior administration official" had been questioned about the IC debate and had dismissed it as a "footnote, not a split." Another unidentified administration official asserted in the same piece that the best "technical experts and nuclear scientists at [weapons] laboratories like Oak Ridge supported the CIA assessments."

That statement was flat-out false, as White House officials well knew, given that the debate had been going on for fifteen months and that the Oak Ridge lab scientists did not support the CIA's assessment at all; they had reached the opposite conclusion.

Q. What happened on the day this article appeared?

A. The Energy Department issued a written order forbidding its scientists to speak publicly about the tubes. Obviously, the Bush administration did not want the public to know that its nuclear experts did not support its position about the use of these tubes.

Q. How was the aluminum-tubes debate covered in the updated NIE that appeared in October 2002?

A. First, I should explain something about the NIE.

Although the NIE is a joint IC document, it is coordinated by the CIA, which is solely responsible for the front section of the NIE. It's called Key Judgments. Regarding nuclear weapons, this section stated that "most agencies" believed Iraq was reconstituting its nuclear-weapons program.

Q. Was that true?

A. No, which I'll explain in a minute. But, in support of its point, the CIA cited Iraq's "aggressive attempts to obtain high-strength aluminum tubes for centrifuge rotors," as well as its attempts to obtain various dual-use equipment, as "compelling evidence" that Saddam Hussein was reconstituting a nuclear-weapons program. Although the CIA tried to gloss over the dispute, the updated NIE that finally appeared in October 2002 did include lengthy dissents about the CIA's position that the tubes were for a nuclear program.

Q. Did the Key Judgments mention any dissents at all?

A. Yes, but only in passing. As to the overall conclusion that "most agencies" believed Iraq had reconstituted its nuclear-weapons programs, the CIA added merely, "see INR alternative view" in parentheses.

The INR alternative view is extremely important to this case, especially as to Colin Powell's speech at the United Nations, because INR, which stands for the Bureau of Intelligence and Research, was the intelligence branch of the Department of State. In other words, the intelligence analysts in Powell's own department did *not* believe that Iraq had reconstituted its nuclear-weapons program.

In a lengthy text box that was not declassified until after

the war began, the State Department analysts noted that the CIA's contention that Iraq was reconstituting its nuclear-weapons program depended on the aluminum-tubes issue. The INR strongly disagreed, however, with the CIA's conclusions about those tubes:

> INR is not persuaded that the tubes in question are intended for use as centrifuge rotors. INR accepts the judgment of technical experts at the U.S. Department of Energy (DOE) who have concluded that the tubes Iraq seeks to acquire are poorly suited for use in gas centrifuges to be used for uranium enrichment and finds unpersuasive the arguments advanced by others to make the case that they are intended for that purpose.

The INR dissent went on to state that it agreed with DOE's assessment that the tubes were likely intended for use in artillery rockets. It then summarized the very same arguments regarding the specifications, the manner of procurement, and Iraq's known efforts to produce rockets that I just went over in detail.

Q. In other words, the defendants were specifically on notice that the CIA's opinion was seriously questioned by the DOE and the State Department, not only because of the fifteen intelligence reports written before September 8, 2002, but also because the DOE's and State Department's reasons for disagreement with the CIA were set forth in the NIE the defendants received in early October 2002?

A. Yes. The October NIE did include a dissent about the tubes by DOE as well. This dissent has never been declassified, but it was discussed at length in the Senate Report.

Q. How did Colin Powell respond to the expert opinions of the DOE nuclear experts and the analysts in his own department?

A. He dismissed them. Throughout the fall of 2002, Powell made numerous misrepresentations about the tubes, and he repeatedly concealed the existence of the educated and well-reasoned assessments of his own intelligence agents and the country's foremost nuclear experts.

His most egregious and calculated deception about the aluminum tubes came, however, during his February 5, 2003, speech to the United Nations. By then, Mohammed El Baradei, the head of the IAEA, had quite publicly joined the chorus of experts denouncing the possibility that the tubes had a nuclear application. On January 8, 2003, he said the IAEA's analysis indicated that the specifications of the tubes sought by the Iraqis "appeared to be consistent with reverse-engineering rockets" and on January 28, he followed up with a more extensive report that reached the same conclusion.

Undaunted by facts, Powell announced:

> Saddam Hussein is determined to get his hands on a nuclear bomb. He is so determined that he has made repeated covert attempts to acquire high-specification aluminum tubes from 11 different countries, even after inspections resumed.

Astoundingly, Powell acknowledged the ongoing controversy but claimed, despite the overwhelming proof to the contrary that had been available since April of 2001:

> Most U.S. experts think they are intended to serve as rotors in centrifuges used to enrich uranium. Other experts, and the Iraqis themselves, argue that they are really to produce the rocket bodies for a conventional weapon, a multiple rocket launcher.

GRAND JUROR: Powell lumped the United States nuclear experts and his own analysts together with the Iraqis?

A. Yes, he did. Powell was deliberately, and quite elaborately, misleading the American public—and the entire world.

Q. We're in the home stretch, people. Let's meet back in ten minutes.

•••

3:20 P.M.

ASSISTANT U.S. ATTORNEY: Agent Crain, when you investigate possible export violations, you occasionally submit affidavits to the court in support of search warrant requests, don't you?

A. Yes, frequently.

Q. Given the intelligence analyses available in September 2002, would you have been able to allege in a search warrant affidavit that these tubes were *really only suitable* for nuclear-centrifuge use?

A. No.

Q. Or that the specifications *proved* that they were intended for a nuclear end-use?

A. No, because neither of those allegations was true.

Q. Well, some agencies had those opinions, didn't they?

A. I don't believe any agency ever stated that the tubes were only really suitable for nuclear-centrifuge use, but even if one agency had offered that opinion, we could not have ignored the others, especially because, the agency with the greatest expertise had reached the opposite conclusion. We're required to present all facts that reasonably relate to an issue, not just ones that help our case for a search warrant.

Q. What would happen if you made such a one-sided allegation in an affidavit?

A. Any evidence found would probably be suppressed in court. I could be disciplined, lose my job, and even be prosecuted for making false statements to the court.

Q. Let's turn to Exhibit 11b. That lists the President's Iraq-related activities for Act Two of WHIG's extravaganza, correct?

A. Yes, it does.

Ex. 11b
Act Two: *Road to Resolution*

SEPTEMBER

9 Remarks by the President and Prime Minister Chrétien on U.S.-Canada Smart Borders [DC]

10 President Bush Holds Roundtable with Arab- and Muslim-American Leaders [DC]

President [and Prime Minister of Portugal] Discuss Mutual Desire to Fight Terror [DC]

Director Ridge, Attorney General Ashcroft Discuss Threat Level [DC]

Statement by the Press Secretary re: Italian Prime Minister's visit

11 President's Remarks to the Nation [New York]

President's Remarks at the Pentagon [DC]

12 President's Remarks at the United Nations General Assembly [New York]

Remarks by the President at United States Reception [New York]

"Iraq: A Decade of Deception and Defiance" [White House website]

13 President discusses Iraq with Reporters [DC]

14 President Discusses Growing Danger Posed by Saddam Hussein's Regime [radio address]

President Bush Meets with Prime Minister of Italy at Camp David

One of the President's central themes for this week was international cooperation, which Ari Fleischer highlighted repeatedly in press briefings. And, of course, on September 12, 2002, the President addressed the United Nations.

Q. Before you testify about that, when Rumsfeld was on *Face the Nation* on September 8, did CBS's Bob Schieffer question his contention that Saddam Hussein presented a threat to the United States?

A. In a sense. Schieffer pointed out that Saddam Hussein had never used WMD against the United States.

Q. What was Rumsfeld's response?

A. He said, "That comment, of course, suggests ought we [*sic*] to wait until he . . . uses them against us. . . . If you go back to September 11, we lost three thousand innocent men, women, and children. Well, if—if you think that's a problem, imagine—imagine a September 11 with weapons of mass destruction."

This hypothetical should be familiar, it's nearly identical to the one that Bush used when he warned about Saddam Hussein in May 2001, except, of course, with the addition of 9/11. It was that very wobbly three-legged argument, which heightened the public's level of fear immensely but had no basis in fact.

Q. This second week was a big one for the fear factor, wasn't it?

A. Yes. These, for example, were the appearances of Bush administration officials on September 9, 2002:

On PBS's *News Hour*, Cheney warned ominously that

we "don't know when" Saddam Hussein will get nuclear weapons. At a press briefing, State Department spokesperson Richard Boucher asked rhetorically, "How long do we wait to find out if [Iraq] has nuclear weapons?"

In an interview with ABC's Sam Donaldson, Defense Department spokesperson Victoria Clarke declared that the "option of doing nothing is off the table," because Saddam Hussein, "with a chemical or biological weapon, could kill tens of thousands of people."

On *Good Morning America*, Rumsfeld cautioned that Iraq was getting closer to nuclear weapons "every day, every week, every month, and therefore time is really not on your side."

Q. During Act Two, how many public appearances did White House officials make where they raised the specter of WMD in the hands of Saddam Hussein?

A. At least thirty-two—and in each such appearance, they referred to 9/11 as well. In fact, during his September 11, 2002, speech from Ellis Island, the President declared, "We will not allow any terrorist or tyrant to threaten civilization with weapons of mass murder," an obvious reference to Saddam Hussein.

Q. In addition to Saddam's violent history, his "continued appetite" for nuclear weapons, and his possession of chemical and biological weapons, what seemed to be the main message of the President's speech to the U.N.?

A. That the UN had to take action—the nature of which was left unspecified—to deal with Saddam's violations of UN resolutions or risk becoming irrelevant.

Q. On September 16, 2002, the Iraqi Minister of Foreign Affairs advised UN Secretary Kofi Annan that Iraq would allow the return of UN weapons inspectors "without conditions." How did the defendants respond to that offer?

A. By all accounts, they were furious. Their objective was a single UN resolution that would not only require the readmission of inspectors but also contain an automatic trigger that would allow the U.S. and its "coalition" to invade Iraq with the U.N.'s blessing without having to seek a second resolution. The more cooperative Iraq appeared to be, the less likelihood the Bush administration had of getting that single resolution, or any resolution.

So, even while they were exhorting the UN to show some backbone, White House officials were parroting Cheney's disparaging description of inspections as providing "false comfort." The President hammered that point home on September 13, 2002, for instance, saying at least four times that he was "doubtful" Saddam Hussein "would meet our demands." The other half of that talking point was that Saddam had already "had 11 years" to comply with UN resolutions.

Q. Did WHIG come up with a written response to Iraq's offer?

A. Yes, almost miraculously, as you can see on Exhibit 11c, the very next day, *Saddam Hussein's Deception and Defiance* appeared on the White House website. Its opening line was: "We've heard 'unconditional' before . . ." The paper then detailed Hussein's history of obstructing inspections.

Q. Could everyone turn to Exhibit 11c?

Ex. 11c
Act Three: *Road to Resolution*

SEPTEMBER

16 President Stresses Budget Discipline and Fiscal Restraint [2002 campaign, Iowa]

Remarks by the President at Jim Nussle for Congress Luncheon [2002 campaign, Iowa]

17 White House website: "Saddam Hussein's Deception & Defiance"

Remarks by the President at Lamar Alexander for Congress Luncheon [2002 campaign, Tennessee]

Remarks by the President on Teaching American History and Civic Education, East Literature Magnet School [2002 campaign, Tennessee]

Statement by the Deputy Press Secretary calling for the United Nations to act despite Iraq's offer of unconditional inspections [White House website]

18 President Discusses Iraq, Domestic Agenda with Congressional Leaders [DC]

19 President Bush to Send Iraq Resolution to Congress Today [White House website]

Remarks by the President at Republican Governors Association Fall Reception [DC]

Remarks by the President After Visit with Employees at Nebraska Avenue Homeland Security Complex [DC]

20 White House website: "National Strategy Report"

Q. The President was back on the campaign trail in this third week?

A. Definitely, and in each of the five appearances, he used the same Rove-inspired MO: raise false fears about Saddam Hussein, link that fear to 9/11, and then promise to protect the American people from this fraudulently crafted threat. See the entry called "President stresses budget discipline and fiscal restraint"? During that speech, the President said the United Nations must act "for the sake of peace" or we would act, because:

> We owe this to our children. . . . Somebody said, well, you know, they don't have a nuclear weapon. I said, well, the most dangerous thing—and we know they're trying to get one—the most dangerous thing would be to find out they had a nuclear weapon after they developed one.
>
> It's a new world we're in. We used to think two oceans could separate us from an enemy. On that tragic day, September the 11th, 2001, we found out that's not the case. We found out this great land of liberty and of freedom and of justice is vulnerable. And therefore we must do everything we can—everything we can—to secure the homeland, to make us safe.

Q. That "two oceans no longer separate us from the enemy" line was one of the President's favorites, wasn't it?

A. Yes, and he usually said it in the course of arguing that we needed to act to protect our children, but during Act Three he actually made those frightening statements *to* children—the grammar-school kids at the magnet school in Tennessee where he spoke on September 17.

Q. What else happened during that third week?

A. Apparently, there'd been enough dialogue, because on September 19, the President, with Colin Powell at his side, announced that he had sent a so-called draft resolution to Congress. He said the resolution included authorization to use force because, "If you want to keep the peace, you've got to have the authorization to use force." Bush insisted that passing the resolution was a "chance for Congress to support me in keeping the peace."

With that announcement, the defendants and the White House Iraq Group moved seamlessly into Act Four, where they ratcheted up the pressure on Congress. Exhibit 11d gives you a good sense of the rising action:

Ex. 11d
Act Four: *Road to Resolution*

SEPTEMBER

23 Remarks by the President at Doug Forrester for Senate Event [2002 campaign, New Jersey]
24 President Urges Congress to Pass Iraq Resolution Promptly [DC]

Remarks by the President at John Thune for Senate Reception [2002 campaign, South Dakota (in DC)]

25 President Bush, Colombia President Uribe Discuss Terrorism

Remarks by the President at the National Republican Senatorial Committee Annual Dinner [2002 campaign, national]

26 President Bush Discusses Iraq with Congressional Leaders [DC]

Remarks by the President at John Cornyn for Senate Reception [2002 campaign, Houston]

27 President Presses Congress for Action on Defense Appropriations Bill [2002 campaign, Denver]

Remarks by the President at Flagstaff, Arizona Welcome [2002 campaign, Flagstaff]

28 President Bush Pushes for Homeland Security Bill [2002 campaign, Phoenix]

Radio Address by President to the Nation re: Iraq [DC]

Q. During week four, how many of the President's speeches focused on the alleged threat from Iraq?

A. Eleven. And seven of which were campaign appearances where he made the same false claims we've discussed and pointedly said that he expected bipartisan support for this resolution.

Q. About that time, former Vice President Al Gore made a public statement about the President's activities, didn't he?

A. He said that President Bush had managed to replace the world's sympathy about 9/11 with fear, anxiety, and uncertainty about Iraq and was using that artificially created threat to steer attention away from his inability to find Bin Laden.

On September 24, 2002, Bush was asked to respond to this comment and he said, "I'm confident a lot of Democrats here in Washington, DC will understand that Saddam is a true threat to America. And I look forward to working with them to get a strong resolution passed."

GRAND JUROR: Were they providing any information directly to Congress?

A. Yes and no. During September, the Bush administration was sending Cheney, Tenet, Rice, Rumsfeld, Powell, and others to speak to members of Congress, both formally and informally, but it had not released any classified information, nor had the updated NIE that Congress requested been released.

So administration officials could issue dire warnings and purport to back them up with "facts," concealing material facts all the while, and Congress had no effective means of questioning them.

On September 19, 2002, for example, Rumsfeld informed the Senate Armed Services Committee: "No terrorist state poses a greater or more immediate threat to the security of our people than the regime of Saddam Hussein." Even if Rumsfeld subjectively believed that claim, it was recklessly false and without any reasonable basis.

For one thing, Saddam Hussein had not taken any aggressive action toward the U.S. since his alleged attempt to assassinate President George H. W. Bush, when Bush was in Kuwait in 1993.

Second, Iraq's military forces and equipment were severely debilitated because of UN sanctions in place since the 1991 Gulf War.

Third, the U.S. intelligence community's classified opinion was that Iraq sponsored only terrorists who were hostile to Israel, not to the United States.

Fourth, the IC's classified assessment was that Iran was the most active state sponsor of terrorism.

Q. Is it fair to say that one of the defendants' frequent talking points was that Iraq posed a "unique" threat among the countries the President had identified as the "axis of evil"?

A. Yes, they had a formulaic explanation for why Iraq was more dangerous than Iran and North Korea, which rested on that rickety three-legged stool.

Q. In early October, the administration received information that completely demolished that weak argument, didn't they?

A. Yes. On approximately October 4, 2002, a State Department representative was specifically informed by North Korean officials that North Korea already possessed nuclear weapons.

Q. Certainly, the President advised Congress and the American public of that significant fact?

A. No. When President Bush made his speech to the nation from Cincinnati, Ohio, on October 7, 2002, he stuck to the script, asserting that Iraq "stands alone" as a unique threat. The Bush administration concealed its knowledge that North Korea had nuclear weapons until October 16, 2002—after Congress had passed the authorization to use military force.

Q. When did the new NIE come out?

A. In order to appreciate the timing of its release, we need to look at Exhibit 11e:

Ex. 11e
Act Five: *Road to Resolution*

OCTOBER

1 Dr. Condoleezza Rice Discusses President's National Security Strategy [New York]

2 President, House Leadership agree on Iraq Resolution [DC]
 The Vice President makes remarks at the NRCC Gala
 Salute to Dick Armey and J. C. Watts [2002 campaign, DC]
 Remarks by the President at Bob Ehrlich for Governor Reception [2002 campaign, Maryland]

3 President Discusses Need for Terrorism Insurance Agreement [DC]
 President Discusses Three Securities [DC]

4 Remarks by the President at Massachusetts Victory 2002 Reception [2002 campaign, Massachusetts]

5 President: Iraqi Regime Danger to America is "Grave and Growing" [radio address]

Remarks by the President at John Sununu for Senate Reception [2002 campaign, New Hampshire]

Remarks by the President in Manchester, New Hampshire, Welcome [2002 campaign, New Hampshire]

Notice the entry for October 2, 2002, "President, House Leadership Agree on Iraq Resolution." That was the day when Congress was scheduled to begin debate on the proposed resolution. White House officials had arranged for the updated NIE to be delivered to both houses of Congress at about 10:00 P.M. on October 1. Even worse, because it was classified, anyone who wanted to read the ninety-page document had to read it in a secure location.

Q. At the same time, there was an unclassified "White Paper" released that purported to summarize the classified version?

A. Yes, and I could spend a whole day talking about it. Suffice it to say, though, that the White Paper presented an entirely false impression of the NIE's assessments, which constituted an egregious fraud upon the public and Congress.

Q. Why?

A. Because even legislators who had time to read the entire document were not allowed, given its highly classified status, to publicly disclose the discrepancies between the two versions in an effort to persuade others in Congress or the American people that the President's arguments were misleading.

Q. Give us a few examples of the discrepancies.

A. The White Paper contained little mention, and no detail, about the serious questions that had been raised by nuclear experts about the aluminum tubes, for starters. There was a similar dispute about unmanned aerial vehicles, or UAVs. The White Paper claimed that Iraq had a UAV that "most analysts" believed was probably intended to deliver biological weapons, but it failed to mention that the U.S. Air Force, the agency with the most expertise on the issue, disagreed with that assessment.

Indeed, almost all dissents were omitted, as were just about any qualifiers that substantially weakened the case for war, such as, "We have low confidence in our ability to assess when Saddam would use WMD." Sometimes words were added to make the case more ominous, as in, "Although Saddam *probably* does not yet have nuclear weapons or sufficient material to make any, he remains intent on acquiring them." The classified NIE asserted outright that Iraq did not have nuclear weapons.

Q. In the end, the majority of members of Congress did find it hard to vote against the resolution, just as the White House Iraq Group leaders had predicted in early September. Isn't that right?

A. Yes. As you can see in Exhibit 11f, the President announced the passage of the resolution on October 16, 2002. This last chart covers a ten-day period:

Ex. 11f
Act Six: *Road to Resolution*

OCTOBER

7 President Outlines Iraqi Threat [national address from Cincinnati]

8 Remarks by the President at Tennessee Welcome [2002 campaign, Tennessee]
Remarks by the President at Van Hilleary for Governor Luncheon [2002 campaign, Tennessee]

10 President Pleased with House Vote on Iraq Resolution [DC]

11 President's Statement on Senate Vote [Passage of Resolution, DC]

12 President's Radio Address to the Nation [re: passage of Iraq resolution]

16 President Signs Iraq Resolution

Q. And on March 18, 2003, the President used that resolution to justify the invasion of Iraq that had been taking place for months?

A. Correct. The resolution was not entirely open-ended. It authorized the use of force only if the President could make certain findings. On March 18, 2003, the President sent a letter to the Speaker of the House of Representatives and the President Pro Tempore of the Senate that mirrored those findings. The letter asserted that:

(1) U.S. reliance on further diplomatic and peace-

> ful means alone would not (a) adequately protect U.S. national security against the "continuing threat posed by Iraq' nor (b) likely lead to enforcement of all relevant UN Security Council resolutions regarding Iraq; and (2) that acting pursuant to the Authorization to Use Military Force was consistent with "continuing to take the necessary actions against international terrorists and terrorist organizations including those nations, organizations or persons who planned, authorized, committed, or aided the terrorists attacks that occurred on September 11, 2001."

Q. Was any part of that letter true?

A. No.

Q. Let's recap what occurred between October 16, 2002, and March 18, 2003. First of all, the President continued to make the same terrifying speech about Iraq right up until the November election, didn't he?

A. Yes, he made the speech at least forty-five times, some days more than once, in Washington, DC, and the following states: Alabama, Arizona, Arkansas, Florida, Georgia, Illinois, Iowa, Kentucky, Maine, Maryland, Minnesota, Missouri, New Hampshire, New Mexico, Pennsylvania, South Dakota, Texas, and West Virginia. I put them in alphabetical order, but Bush actually bounced all over the place and returned to several states three or four times.

Q. The President was able to manipulate the electorate and

get Congress on board, but in order to keep everyone on board, he had a problem, didn't he?

A. Yes. Iraq had readmitted the UN inspectors in November 2002, which was causing two problems: Although the inspection process was not entirely smooth, Saddam Hussein was basically cooperating, so the "wrong-footing" strategy was not working very well; but also the inspectors were not finding any WMD.

Q. How did the President and his advisers respond to that?

A. They just kept repeating their talking points. They also revived ones that they had been specifically warned were unreliable. Most famously, in his January 28, 2003, State of the Union address, Bush announced that the "British have recently learned that Iraq was seeking significant quantities of uranium from Africa."

Much has been written regarding what the President knew when he made this statement, but the analysis of whether this statement is fraudulent in a criminal context is very simple. As the grand jurors have heard at length, this President is highly involved with the speech-writing process. At the time of this speech, the public's support for the war was waning and the President wanted specific proof. If he could have phrased this assertion more strongly, he would have. It may have been literally true—the British did acquire this information—but it had already been debunked. Bush's phrasing was an attempt to deceive the American public into believing that he was vouching for the British intelligence information when he knew he could not do so, while still allowing himself that old stand-by, plausible deniability.

Q. So, on March 18, 2003, did the defendants have any more reason to believe that Saddam Hussein was linked to the attacks of September 11, 2001, than they had on September 12, 2001?

A. No.

Q. Did they have any more reason to believe that Saddam Hussein's regime was involved with al Qaeda?

A. No. The IC had said all along that there was no ongoing collaborative relationship.

Q. Did they have any solid evidence whatsoever that Saddam Hussein had weapons of mass destruction?

A. No, nor did they have any evidence that he wanted to attack the United States. The CIA's opinion, which was completely ignored by the defendants, was that "Baghdad for now appears to be drawing a line short of conducting terrorist attacks with conventional or CBW against the Unite States."

Q. CBW are chemical and biological weapons?

A. Yes. The CIA did not believe Iraq had nuclear weapons.

Q. Under what scenario did the CIA believe that Saddam might actually attack the United States?

A. If he knew for certain that we were going to attack him.

Q. Was it even true that Saddam Hussein was not cooperating with the inspections?

A. No, the UN weapons inspectors were practically pleading with the United States to allow the process to continue.

Q. Special Agent Crain, the day after Bush issued an ultimatum to Saddam Hussein, an article by William Kristol appeared in *The Weekly Standard*, did it not?

A. Yes, which is the magazine that published an issue entitled "Saddam Must Go" years before. Kristol is one of its editors, a Project for a New American Century member and a long-time vocal proponent of forcibly removing Saddam Hussein. After lauding the "courage" of George W. Bush and Tony Blair in deciding to invade Iraq, Kristol wrote:

> Obviously, we are gratified that the Iraq strategy we have long advocated—and whose contours were further specified in that December 1, 1997, issue, in articles by Zalmay Khalilzad and Paul Wolfowitz, Frederick W. Kagan, and Peter Rodman—has become the policy of the U.S. government, because we believe it is the right policy.

Q. So Bush, Cheney, Libby, Wolfowitz, and the many proponents of the PNAC principles with whom they allied themselves got their wish, didn't they?

A. Yes, they did.

Q. What has been the cost of this conspiracy to defraud the United States?

A. Almost 2,600 American soldiers killed up to now, at least 19,000 wounded, many more than 50,000 Iraqis killed, and unknown numbers—hundreds of thousands—wounded and homeless. Government funds? Over $350 billion in direct costs and spiraling upward daily.

The betrayal of the American people? How do you put a number on the loss of trust that Wilton Sekzer described in *Why We Fight*:

> I'm from the old school and for me certain people walk on water, and the President of the United States is one of them. If I can't trust the President of the United States, I don't know. It's a terrible thing, when American citizens can't trust their president. . . . The government exploited my feelings of patriotism, of a deep desire for revenge for what happened to my son.

How do you put a number on Wilton Sekzer's loss? Or that of hundreds of thousands of people who have lost sons, daughters, husbands, wives, brothers, sisters, mothers, and fathers. How do you put a number on the loss of America's good will in the world? The total loss from this fraud will probably never be known. It is unimaginable.

Q. Members of the jury. That brings us to the close of the evidence. I want to remind you of the legal issue that you must now decide.

Keep in mind that the *only* question before you is whether, as to each defendant, there is probable cause to believe that he or she committed the crime charged in the indictment. Probable cause means "sufficient facts and circumstances to allow a reasonable person to conclude that something is true."

You do not have to decide whether all of the defendants are equally culpable or whether they all became members of the conspiracy at the same time. You do not have to decide whether these defendants are the *only* people who conspired to defraud the United States by deceiving the public and Congress about prewar intelligence on Iraq. Clearly, they are not. But the fact that additional people could or should be charged with a crime does not provide a defense to those who *are* charged.

Similarly, it is of no moment that President Bush is not the only American president who has deceived the public about war. We know that he is not. But it's no defense to a crime that someone else, at some other time, committed the same crime.

And finally, as to the Project for a New American Century principles of a bold foreign policy, preventive attacks to protect against possible threats and to secure our access to oil in the Middle East. It is entirely possible—indeed, even probable—that most of the defendants sincerely believed, and continue to believe, that the United States would be better off if we followed those principles. In other words, it is entirely possible that the defendants thought that the achievement of their ultimate goal would benefit not just Americans but the entire world.

The issue is not whether the President or his advisers sincerely believed that. You may assume that they did. Nor is the issue whether those beliefs are valid, or morally justified, or wise. Some of you may disagree with them; some of you may agree. Certainly, we are all relieved that Saddam Hussein is gone. But this case is not about the

President's foreign-policy beliefs or whether the invasion of Iraq was a good or bad strategic decision.

The case is about whether the President and his most senior advisers deceived people in order to achieve their goal. The law of fraud is very clear: a defendant's honest belief that a venture will ultimately succeed is not a defense to fraud, if in carrying out the venture, he knowingly makes fraudulent representations intended to deceive others.

In other words, you can't mislead people to get them to do what you want them to do, or to think what you want them to think, even if you believe that what you're trying to get them to do or think is for their own good.

It's also possible, even probable, that the President and some of his senior aides actually believed that Saddam Hussein had some WMD. But the issue is not whether they sincerely held such a belief or assessment and were merely mistaken. The issue is whether they deceived the public and Congress to make their case stronger. In other words, the sole legal question for you to decide is this:

> Is there probable cause to believe that George W. Bush, Richard B. Cheney, Donald M. Rumsfeld, Condoleezza Rice, Colin Powell, and others used deceit, craft, trickery, dishonest means—including lies, false pretenses, misrepresentations, deliberate omissions, half-truths, false promises and statements made with reckless indifference to their truth—to obstruct, impede, or interfere with Congress' lawful government function of overseeing foreign affairs, relating to the invasion of Iraq?

Agent Crain and I will leave now to allow you to vote on the indictment. Thank you for your service.

•••

END OF DAY SEVEN

A FINAL WORD

Is *United States v. George W. Bush et al.* an exact depiction of a grand jury presentation? In the words of Special Agent Campbell: "Yes and no."

It is not uncommon for grand jurors to make comments and ask questions. They usually raise their hands, but complete verisimilitude in that regard would have been quite tedious. Grand juries take their responsibilities extremely seriously, yet they *are* human. Any group of twenty-five people spending eight hours together once a week for eighteen months develops its own dynamic. Not surprisingly, then, grand jurors become friends, get on each others' nerves, engage in corny banter, and occasionally complain—particularly about the room temperature and federal cafeteria fare.

Of course, *this* grand jury is hypothetical, but the presentation does follow the format that other federal prosecutors and I routinely used in grand jury proceedings. In complicated cases—even, most likely, a case such as this—outside witnesses may be called to testify about the events they were involved in, especially if the prosecutor is concerned that a cooperator might "go south" (in other words, change his story later on). In the majority of instances, however, the evidence is presented through summary testimony by investigative agents just like fictional agents Campbell, Estrada, and Crain.

If this particular grand jury is hypothetical and the agents fictional, the facts presented are neither. As any prosecutor would attest, an accusation of criminal wrongdoing—official or unofficial—should never be made lightly, nor should it be based on fiction or hypothesis. Therefore, the facts set out in this book have been carefully researched and are, quite tragically, all too real. The legal principles I've explained are similarly real, based on federal statutes and well-established case law.

Applying this long-settled law to these incontrovertible facts leads, unfortunately, to but a single conclusion: the President and his aides did, in fact, conspire to defraud the United States by deceiving the nation and Congress about the grounds for an invasion of Iraq. Based solely on fiction and hypothesis, they caused the most powerful nation in the world to attack another, virtually powerless, country comprised largely of innocent men, women, and children who had the horrifying misfortune of being ruled by a merciless dictator.

Turning back to the Enron trial one final time, consider Prosecutor Katherine Ruemmler's closing argument. The investors and employees of Enron, she said,

> [r]elied on the accuracy and the integrity and the fullness and completeness of the information being given by the CEOs of the company. These people who were not privileged enough to be in the inner circle . . . were deprived of the opportunity

> to make their own choices about what to do with their Enron stock . . .
>
> [T]hey were the owners of Enron. It was their Enron. It wasn't Mr. Lay's Enron. It wasn't Mr. Skillings's Enron. It was their Enron. They were entitled to know the truth about what was going on at the company so they could make the choices that they needed to make with their money and their stock.

Can there be any question that the same holds true in this case? There is not one set of facts for people inside the Oval Office and another for people outside the Oval Office. It is not President Bush's United States. It is not Vice President Cheney's United States. It is not Rumsfeld's or Rice's or Powell's United States. Our government officials are elected to serve the American people: it is the American people's United States.

We, the American people, relied on the truthfulness, integrity, fullness, and completeness of the information about Iraq that the President provided to us. We were, just like the Enron fraud victims, entitled to honest information; we were entitled to know the truth about Iraq so we could make informed choices about our lives, how our money was to be used, whether and where our children, parents, spouses, siblings, cousins, and friends were to be sent into battle, and the actions of our country in the world—the actions being taken in our names.

The President, the Vice President, and their most senior advisers have perpetrated a massive fraud upon our country. Their crime was—and continues to be—far worse than the Enron fraud. We must not shrug our shoulders and walk away.

Elizabeth de la Vega
Los Gatos, California
August 14, 2006

ACKNOWLEDGMENTS

Profound and heartfelt thanks go to Tom Engelhardt, my incisive editor and extraordinarily patient mentor, who launched this book and navigated it to the safe harbor of Seven Stories Press, somehow managing to act as beacon and ballast all the while. This book truly would not exist without his guidance and inspiration.

I am most appreciative of Dan Simon and the staff at Seven Stories Press, who enthusiastically adopted this project and completed it at warp speed. I am equally grateful to Louise Fili for the extraordinary cover design.

This book is also inspired by the soldiers, federal employees, grieving family members, reporters, and writers who have dared to seek and tell the truth about the actions of the Bush-Cheney administration. Most I have only been able to admire from afar, awed by their courage, intelligence, and accomplishments, but in researching this book I had the pleasure of speaking with cofounder of Iraq Veterans Against the War Tim Goodrich and (Ret.) Lt. Colonel Karen Kwiatkowski, for whose time, insights, and delightful company I am extremely grateful.

Family, neighbors, and friends old and new—from the chiropractor's office to the Internet, from Boston to the Bay Area—have cheered from the sidelines. Carol A. and Debbie J., Cynthia, Joan, Jeanne, Mary Jo, Carol N., Lynn and Susan, Karen, Tricia, Mary C., and my not-so-little-anymore Joanna, the value of your support and friendship is immeasurable. Linda and Yonkel not only offered writing expertise, but kept me laughing.

Finally, of course, to Chris, Danny, Shannon, Lindsay, Evan, and my beloved Paul, thank you for putting up with me during this whirlwind experience. Let's all just put that washer-dryer incident behind us.

NOTES

INTRODUCTION: A FRAUD WORSE THAN ENRON

"Committee on Intelligence": *Report of the Select Committee on Intelligence on the U.S. Intelligence Community's Prewar Intelligence Assessments on Iraq*, Senate Report 108–301 ("The Senate Report") (U.S. Government Printing Office, July 9, 2004).

"9/11 Commission": *Final Report of the National Commission on Terrorist Attacks Upon the United States* ("The 9/11 Report") (New York: W.W. Norton, 2004).

"Barbara Olshansky, David Lindorff": David Lindorff and Barbara Olshansky, *The Case for Impeachment* (New York: Thomas Dunne Books, 2006).

"John Dean": John Dean, *Worse than Watergate: The Secret Presidency of George W. Bush* (Boston: Little, Brown & Co., 2003).

"Michael Ratner": Center for Constitutional Rights, *Articles of Impeachment Against George W. Bush* (Hoboken: Melville Publishing, 2006).

"Elizabeth Holtzman": Elizabeth Holtzman, "The Impeachment of George W. Bush," *The Nation* (January 30, 2006).

"to see Justice Done": "Prosecution: Lay Testimony Helped Our Case," ABC News (May 26, 2006), http://abcnews.go.com/GMA/LegalCenter/story?id=2007526&page=1.

"one night in 1964": Malcolm Gladwell, *The Tipping Point* (New York: Little, Brown, & Company, 2002), 28.

"really a problem": Id.

"heard her scream": Id.

"suite in this country": White House, *President Bush Signs Corporate Crime Bill* (July 30, 2006). (All White House press briefings and presidential speeches referenced throughout this work are available at http://www.whitehouse.gov.)

"Sarbanes-Oxley Act": Sarbanes-Oxley Act of 2002, PL 107–204, 116 Stat 745 (2002).

"United States Code, Section 371": The indictment in *U.S.* v. *Skilling et. al.* is available at http://images.chron.com/content/news/photos/06/05/18/final-redactedindictmentforjury.pdf.

"as outright lies": Jury instructions from *U.S. v. Skilling* are available at http://images.chron.com/content/news/photos/06/05/15/juryinstructions1.pdf.

"child gets lost": Shaheen Pasha and Jessica Seid, "Lay and Skillings' Day of Reckoning," CNN News Online (May 25, 2005), http://money.cnn.com/2006/05/25/newsmakers/Enron_verdict/index.htm.

"on honest information": White House, *President Bush Signs Corporate Crime Bill.*

"so particularly susceptible": United States Sentencing Guidelines, Sect. 3A1.1 (2005).

DAY ONE

"pretenses or representations": This and all future references to jury instructions are from Edward J. Devitt, Blackmar and Kevin F. O'Malley, *Federal Jury Practice and Instructions: Criminal, Fourth Edition* (St. Paul: West Publishing Co., 1990).

"bold foreign policy": "The War Behind Closed Doors: Excerpts from Draft "Defense Planning Guidance," *Frontline* (March 2003), http://www.pbs.org/wgbh/pages/frontline/shows/iraq/etc/wolf.html.

"Hussein from power": Project for a New American Century, *Letter to President William J. Cinton* ("PNAC Letter to Clinton") (January 26, 1998), http://www.newamericancentury.org.

"a new Pearl Harbor": Report of the Project for a New American Century, *Rebuilding America's Defenses* (September 2000), http://www.newamerican-century.org/RebuildingAmericasDefenses.pdf.

"nuclear weapons program": The Senate Report 84.

"for invading Iraq": Details in this and following paragraphs regarding the Bush administration's war planning can be found in Bob Woodward, *Plan of Attack* (New York: Simon & Schuster, 2004).

"and his advisers": The Downing Street Memos referenced throughout this work can be found at http://downingstreetmemo.com/.

"to this joint resolution": The text of the October 11, 2002, Joint Resolution is available at *PBS*'s *NewsHour* website, http://www.pbs.org/newshour/bb/middle_east/july-dec02/joint_resolution_10-11-02.html.

"U.S. intelligence agencies": Citations for "Overt Acts" alleged in the hypothetical indictment will be referenced as they appear in the hypothetical grand jury presentation that follows.

"conspiracy at Enron": "Closing Argument by Katherine Ruemmler in trial of *U.S.* v. *Skilling*" ("Ruemmler Closing Argument"), Chron.com, Special Report (May 15, 2006), http://images.chron .com/content/news/photos/06/05/16/closing_goverment.pdf.

"advising trial juries": Jury instructions referenced throughout this work are derived from *Federal Jury Practice*, cited above.

"merging with Enron": Cross-examination by John Hueston in *U.S. v. Skilling*, Chron.com, Special Report (May 1, 2006), http://images .chron.com/content/news/photos/06/05/01/transcript_0501_lay2.pdf.

DAY TWO

"you're a liar": Wilton Sekzer, quoted in *Why We Fight*, directed by Eugene Jarecki, http://www.sonyclassics.com/whywefight/main.html.

"and Saddam Hussein": David Corn, *The Lies of George W. Bush* (New York: Three Rivers Press, 2003), 324.

"to remove Saddam Hussein": Karen Kwiatkoski, "The New Pentagon Papers," *Salon* (March 10, 2004), http://dir.salon.com/ story/opinion/feature/2004/03/10/osp_moveon/index1.html?pn=1.

"1997 Wall Street Journal": David Wurmser, "Iraq Needs a Revolution," *Wall Street Journal* (November 12, 1997), http://www.aei.org/news/newsID.8361/news_detail.asp.

"Tehran and Gaza": David Wurmser, "Middle East War," *Washington Times* (November 1, 2000).

"they become dire": Project for a New American Century Web site (1997), http://www.newamericancentury.org/.

"rid of him": Zalmay Khalilzad and Paul Wolfowitz, "Overthrow Him," *Weekly Standard* (December 1, 1997).

"UN Security Council": PNAC Letter to Clinton.

"regime of Saddam Hussein": *Rebuilding America's Defenses.*

"a new Pearl Harbor": Id.

"taking down governments": *Meet the Press* (NBC television broadcast, August 27, 2000).

"as nation-builders": First Bush-Gore Presidential Debate (October 3, 2000), http://www.debates.org/pages/trans2000a.html.

"that promotes freedom": Second Bush-Gore Presidential Debate (October 11, 2000), http://www.debates.org/pages/ trans2000b.html.

"resoluting [*sic*] your determination": Republican Primary Debate (December 2, 1999), http://www.vote-smart.org/speech_detail.php?speech_id=3039.

"are as well": Id.

"Commander-in-Chief": "McCain Vows End to Attack Ads, Urges Bush to do Same," CNN.com (February 11, 2000), http://archives.cnn.com/2000/ALLPOLITICS/stories/02/11/campaign.wrap/.

"a successful presidency": Russ Baker, *Bush Wanted to Invade Iraq if Elected in 2000*, GNN.TV (October 24, 2004), http://www.gnn.tv/articles/article.php?id=761.

DAY THREE

"priority was Iraq": Michael R. Gordon and General Bernard E. Trainor, *Cobra II: The Inside Story of the Invasion and Occupation of Iraq* (New York: Pantheon Books, 2006), 13–14.

"a wild card": "Bush Sees Saddam as 'Big Threat,' May use Force," Reuters (January 19, 2001), http://archive.gulfnews.com/articles/01/01/19/7326.html.

"occurred to us": *This Week* (ABC television broadcast, February 4, 2001).

"got his attention": "U.S., British Planes Attack Iraqi Targets," Reuters (February 16, 2001), http://www.commondreams.org/headlines01/0216-03.htm.

"no longer enough": White House, *Remarks by President to Students and Faculty at National Defense University* (May 1, 2001).

"*Bush at War*": White House, *Ask the White House* (May 2, 2003).

"activity after 9/11": Such references not yet cited in these enotes include: John Prados, *Hood-Winked* (New York: The New Press, 2004); Ron Suskind, *The One Percent Doctrine* (New York: Simon & Schuster, 2006); Paul Thompson, *The Terror Timeline: Year by Year, Day by Day, Minute by Minute*, (New York: HarperCollins Publishers Inc., 2004), *Misled into War*, DowningSt.com, http://www.downingstreetmemo.com/timelinehome.html.

"in any way": Richard Clarke, *Against All Enemies* (New York: Free Press, 2004), 30.

"been about Iraq": Ron Suskind, *The Price of Loyalty: George W. Bush, the White House, and the Education of Paul O'Neill* (New York: Simon and Schuster, 2004).

"views and opinions": White House, *Press Briefing by Scott McClellan* (January 14, 2004).

"to get a good case": A copy of the original note is available at http://www.flickr.com/photos/66726692@N00/100545349/.

DAY FOUR

"Commander-in-Chief": White House, *President Shares Thanksgiving Meal with Troops* (November 21, 2001).

"place in Afghanistan": White House, *President, General Franks Discuss War Effort* (December 28, 2001).

"an invasion of Iraq": The 9/11 Commission Report, 330 et. seq.

"what the others thought": *Plan of Attack*, 251.

"to civilization itself": White House, *President Bush Meets with German Chancellor Schroeder* (May 23, 2002).

"everything we've found": *U.S. v. Skilling et. al.* indictment.

"desk right now": White House, *President Bush Meets with Australian Prime Minister* (June 13, 2002).

"plan to him": *Nightline* (ABC television broadcast, July 15, 2002).

"is briefing today": White House, *Press Briefing by Ari Fleischer* (September 3, 2002).

"to the contrary": Dana Millbank, "For President, Facts are Malleable," *Washington Post* (October 11, 2002).

DAY FIVE

"in the region": *NewsHour* (PBS television broadcast, March 11, 2002).

"action against Iraq": Id.

"friends and allies": Id.

"of you respond?": White House, *President Welcomes Prime Minister Tony Blair to the White House* (June 6, 2005).

"take military action": Id.

"of his race": Id.

"deal with Saddam": Id.

"Downing Street Memo": All Downing Street Memos referred to herein can be found at http://downingstreetmemo.com/docs.

"go into Iraq": White House, *Press Briefing by Scott McClellan* (May 16, 2005).

"with the threat": White House, *President Bush Discusses Foreign Policy with Congressional Leaders* (September 4, 2002).

"out of them": Eric Herter, "Iraq War Presence in D.C. Unreported," *Common Dreams News Center*, http://www.commondreams.org/views05/0926-31.htm.

DAY SIX

"nuclear weapons program": The Senate Report, 84 et. seq.

"into the war": "The Dark Side," *Frontline* (PBS television broadcast, June 26, 2006), http://www.pbs.org/wgbh/pages/frontline/darkside/view/.

"for a public case": Id.

"to support terror": White House, *President Delivers State of the Union Address* (January 29, 2002).

"over a decade": Id.

"their dead children": Id.

"the civilized world": Id.

"would be catastrophic": Id.

"pretty well confirmed": *Meet the Press* (NBC television broadcast, December 9, 2001).

"to bank account": The 9/11 Commission Report.

"beyond a reasonable doubt": Department of Defense, *Wolfowitz Interview with the San Francisco Chronicle*, http://www.defenselink.mil/transcripts/2002/t02272002_t0223sf.html.

"proof of it": Memorandum from Christopher Meyer, U.K. Ambassador to U.S., to David Manning, U.K. Foreign Policy Advisor (March 18, 2002).

"do with [9/11]": Karen Kwiatkowski, "Bush Administration Achieves Scientific Breakthrough: Time Travel Mastered!" LewRockwell.com (2003), http://www.lewrockwell.com/kwiatkowski/kwiatkowski32.html.

"in his box": White House, *Vice President Speaks at 103rd National Convention* (August 26, 2002).

"communications and speechwriting": Laura Flanders, *Bushwomen: Tales of a Cynical Species* (New York: Verso Books, 2004).

"vote against it": Elisabeth Bumiller, "Traces of Terror: The Strategy; Bush Aides Set Strategy to Sell Policy on Iraq," *New York Times* (September 7, 2002).

DAY SEVEN

"Exhibit 11a through 11f": All White House appearances listed on Exhibits a through 11f are listed verbatim as they appear at http://www.whitehouse.gov.

"to do anything": White House, *President Discusses Foreign Policy with Congressional Leaders* (September 4, 2002).

"of mass destruction": White House, *Remarks by the President at Bob Ehrlich for Governor Reception* (October 2, 2002).

"obtained such material": Joseph Curl, "Agency Disavows Report on Iraq Arms," *Washington Times* (September 27, 2002).

"pre-Iraq war intelligence": Details cited in this section on aluminum tubes pre-war intelligence can be found in The Senate Report, 84–124 and the Report of the Robb-Silberman Commission, Notes 24–71, available at http://www.wmd.gov/ report/index.html.

"them the tubes": The Senate Report 112.

"aluminum tubes allegations": For an excellent analysis on this topic, see Barton Gellman and Walter Pincus, "Depiction of Threat Outgrew Supporting Evidence," *Washington Post* (August 10, 2003). For a detailed chronology see the series by eriposte, "WMDgate: Fixing Intelligence Around Policy," *The Left Coaster*, http://www.theleftcoaster.com/archives/006022.php.

"the opposite conclusion": The Senate Report 94.

"about the tubes": "Energy Dept Tells Scientists to Hush on Iraq," Secrecy News, http://www.fas.org/sgp/news/secrecy/2002/10/ 101502.html.

"Key Judgments": For a comparison of the CIA's October 2002 publicly-released "Key Judgments" to the information declassified in July 2003, see http://www.aph.gov.au/house/committee/pjcaad/WMD/report/appendixf.pdf.

"for that purpose": A detailed analysis of the NIE and its dissenting opinions about the tubes is in The Senate Report 94–124.

"reverse-engineering rockets": "Status of the Agency's Verification Activities in Iraq As of 8 January 2003 by IAEA Director General Dr. Mohamed ElBaradei," IAEA.org, http://www.iaea.org/NewsCenter/Statements/2003/ebsp2003n002.shtmlat.

"after inspections resumed": White House, *Secretary of State Colin Powell Addresses the U.N.* (February 5, 2003), http://www.whitehouse.gov/news/releases/2003/02/20030205-1.html.

"to the court": "Former Federal Prosecutor and State Department Agent Indicted for Obstruction of Justice and Presenting False Evidence in Terrorism Trial," Department of Justice Press Release (March 29, 2006), http://justice.gov/criminal/press_room/press_releases/2006_4530_3-29-06Convertino.pdf.

"of mass destruction": *Face the Nation* (CBS television broadcast, September 8, 2002).

"don't know when": *NewsHour* (PBS television broadcast, September 9, 2002).

"has nuclear weapons": Department of Defense, *Daily Press Briefing by Richard Boucher* (September 9, 2002), http://www.state.gov/r/pa/prs/dpb/2002/13344.htm.

"thousands of people": Department of Defense, *ASD PA Clarke Interview with Sam Donaldson* (September 9, 2002), http://www.defenselink .mil/transcripts/2002/sep2002.html.

"on your side": *Good Morning America*, (ABC television broadcast, September 9, 2002).

"meet our demands": White House, *President Discusses Iraq with Reporters* (September 13, 2002).

"heard 'unconditional' before": White House, *Saddam Hussein's Deception and Defiance* (September 17, 2002).

"make us safe": White House, *President Bush Discusses Budget Discipline and Fiscal Restraint* (September 16, 2002).

"on September 17th": White House, *Remarks by the President on Teaching American History and Civic Education East Literature Magnet School* (September 17, 2002).

"keeping the peace": White House, *President Bush to Send Iraq Resolution to Congress Today* (September 19, 2002).

"to find Bin Laden": Vice President Al Gore, *Speech to the Commonwealth Club* (September 23, 2002), http://www.usatoday.com/news/nation/2002-09-23-gore-text_x.htm.

"strong resolution passed": White House, *President Urges Congress to Pass Iraq Resolution Promptly* (September 24, 2002).

"of Saddam Hussein": Donald Rumsfeld, *Testimony before the Senate Armed Services Committee Regarding Iraq* (published September 19, 2002), http://www.defenselink.mil/speeches/2002/s20020919-secdef2.html.

"use military force": Andrea Koppel and John King, *U.S.: North Korea Admits Nuke Program*, CNN.com. (October 17, 2002), http://archives.cnn.com/2002/US/10/16/us.nkorea/.

"have nuclear weapons": Jessica Tuchman Matthews, "A Tale of Two Intelligence Estimates," http://www.carnegieendowment.org/publications/index.cfm?fa=view&id=1489.

"September 11, 2001": White House, *Text of a Letter from the President to the Speaker of the House of Representatives and the President Pro Tempore of the Senate* (March 18, 2003).

"uranium from Africa": White House, *President Delivers State of the Union*, (January 28, 2003).

"the right policy": William Kristol, "Finally Saddam Hussein will be Forced off the World's Stage," *Weekly Standard* (March 17, 2003).

"to my son": Sekzer, quoted in *Why We Fight*.

A FINAL WORD

"and their stock": Ruemmler Closing Argument.

ABOUT THE AUTHOR

Elizabeth de la Vega is a native of Needham, Massachusetts, who has migrated west through Michigan and Minnesota and now lives in Northern California. A federal prosecutor for twenty-one years, she was an Assistant U.S. Attorney in Minneapolis, as well as a member of the Organized Crime Strike Force and Branch Chief in San Jose. Since her retirement in 2004, Ms. de la Vega has been a regular contributor to TomDispatch. Her articles have also appeared in *The Nation*, the *Los Angeles Times*, the *Christian Science Monitor*, *Salon*, and *Mother Jones*.

ABOUT TOMDISPATCH.COM

TomDispatch.com began in November 2001 as Tom Engelhardt's unnamed e-list of commentary and collected articles from the world press. In December 2002 it gained its name, became a project of The Nation Institute, and went online as "a regular antidote to the mainstream media." It now posts Tom Engelhardt's regular commentaries and the original work of authors ranging from Rebecca Solnit and Mike Davis to Chalmers Johnson, Michael Klare, and the author of this book, Elizabeth de la Vega. TomDispatch is intended to introduce readers to voices and perspectives from elsewhere (even when the elsewhere is here). Its mission is to connect some of the global dots regularly left unconnected by the mainstream media and to offer a clearer sense of how this imperial globe of ours actually works. Tom Engelhardt, consulting editor for Metropolitan Books and cofounder of its American Empire Project series, is the author of *The End of Victory Culture*, a history of American "triumphalism" in the Cold War, and most recently, *Mission Unaccomplished, Tomdispatch Interviews with American Iconoclasts and Dissenters* (Natio[illegible]

ABOU[illegible]

Seven Stories Pr[illegible] ıblisher based in New Yor[illegible] ıout the United States, C[illegible] Ve publish works of the [illegible] Nelson Algren, Octavia [illegible] ɔrfman, Lee Stringer, and [illegible] ɔgether with political title[illegible] ing the Boston Women[illegible] Noam Chomsky, Ralph [illegible] nsored, Barbara Seaman, [illegible] among many others. Our [illegible] erback, pamphlet, and e-b[illegible] panish. We believe publishers have a special responsibility to defend free speech and human rights wherever we can.

For more information about us, visit our Web site at www.sevenstories.com or write for a free catalogue to Seven Stories Press, 140 Watts Street, New York, NY 10013.